THIS IS A BORZOI BOOK
PUBLISHED BY ALFRED A. KNOPF, INC.

Copyright © 1992 by Eric Bettelheim and
Alvin A Rosenfeld
All rights reserved under International and
Pan-American Copyright Conventions. Published
in the United States by Alfred A. Knopf, Inc.,
New York, and simultaneously in Canada by
Random House of Canada Limited, Toronto.
Distributed by Random House, Inc., New York.

Library of Congress Cataloging-in-Publication Data
Bettelheim, Bruno.
The art of the obvious / by Bruno Bettelheim and Alvin A
Rosenfeld.—1st ed.
p.   cm.
Includes index.
ISBN 0-679-40029-X
1. Psychotherapy.   2. Psychoanalysis.   3. Psychotherapy
—Case studies.   I. Rosenfeld, Alvin A.   II. Title.
[DNLM: 1. Psychotherapy—methods.   WM 420 B565]
RC480.5.B468   1993
616.89'14—dc20
DNLM/DLC
for Library of Congress   92-54281
CIP

Manufactured in the United States of America
FIRST EDITION

To our beloved wives,

in memory of Trude Weinfeld Bettelheim,

in honor of Dorothy Levine Rosenfeld,

and with gratitude to our students,

and to our best teachers, our patients

CONTENTS

PREFACE

THIS BOOK PRESENTS an approach to learning to practice psychotherapy. But it also reflects a collaboration that began after I became affiliated with the Child Psychiatry Division at Stanford University Medical School and moved, in 1977, to the San Francisco Bay Area where Bruno Bettelheim had retired. I was privileged to work closely with Bettelheim and to become his friend despite the difference in our ages—when we met, he was seventy-four, I was thirty-two.

Soon after I came to Stanford, I invited Bettelheim to join me in teaching a weekly seminar in psychotherapy for therapists in training or in practice. We spent a good deal of time together, discussing privately what had transpired in the given week's session, and speaking about my patients and our concerns. After I left Stanford, our collaboration continued and our friendship deepened. For the rest of my life, I will cherish the time we spent together.

Over his long career, Bruno Bettelheim led hundreds of individual teaching sessions dealing with psychotherapy. In our six years together at Stanford, we conducted well over one hundred sessions in a weekly seminar open to students in child and adult psychiatry, psychology, and social work. Practitioners in the community also attended from time to time. The sessions were lively, thought-provoking, and humorous, and at times involved a tense, even testy, yet vital exchange of ideas on issues that concerned Bettelheim deeply.

From the first, we encouraged participants to bring particularly difficult cases to the seminar, cases with which they needed help that they were not getting elsewhere. It was clear to me at our very first seminar that Bettelheim was a brilliant and virtuoso teacher of psychotherapy. When I tried out some of his ideas and techniques with my patients, I found them to be far more effective than many of my own carefully thought-over methods. But the coherence of his approach was not immediately apparent; it took me some time to grasp the attitude and thinking that underlay it. When I understood his approach more clearly, I saw that it was unique, and after a couple of years, I found myself incorporating it into my own.

Although Bettelheim wrote many extraordinary books, I feel that none of them comes close to presenting the sort of free exchange of ideas on how to deal with a psychotherapeutic patient that I experienced in these seminars. Over the time I knew Bettelheim, I grew to think that this approach to teaching students about psychotherapy ought to be shared with others in book form. The purpose would be to present Bettelheim's and my ideas as a useful tool for psychotherapists and psychotherapy students. Because Bettelheim's insights were so universal in character, I also felt that they would interest a wider audience.

Although Bettelheim was willing to let me attempt the project, he was extremely skeptical. He had been disappointed by the failure of his 1962 book *Dialogues with Mothers* to attract as broad an audience as he had hoped for, and he attributed this failure in large part to its form. If I remember correctly, he said that the last book of dialogues to win a wide readership had been Plato's. No book, he felt, could remotely capture the feeling of a seminar or teach the way a seminar could.

What transpired in the sessions needed to be edited down to its essence, clarified, rearranged, supplemented, made more concise. I wanted to transform the material into something that was as alive on paper as it had been in reality; I wanted to give an accurate impression of what it was like to sit in several years of seminars with Bruno Bettelheim.

From the outset I realized that most readers would find it tedious to wade through verbatim transcriptions of seminars and decided that the book should in no way seek to present an exact factual record of given sessions. I therefore selected parts from many different sessions that dealt with the same or related subjects, and then stitched them together and added narrative seams to create a composite.

By that time I had moved to New York City, and Bettelheim and I lived a continent apart. When I sent him my earliest efforts, he began, to his surprise and delight, to see that the project *could* work. With the generous support of the Rockefeller Foundation, Bettelheim and I worked together in August of 1985, at Villa Serballoni, the foundation's study center in Bellagio on Lake Como, Italy. We experimented with various ways of presenting this material, but in the end were satisfied that the reconstituted seminars made sophisticated, sometimes subtle, ideas far more accessible to the reader. In our collaborative efforts that month, we reflected more deeply on those ideas, and as a result the material was expanded and acquired a new resonance and depth which would not have always been apparent in the fast-moving, often digressive, seminars as they actually transpired.

In the presentation of psychotherapeutic work, protecting a patient's confidentiality is an obvious necessity. Because, as was characteristic of Bettelheim's approach, these sessions often focused not just on the patient's emotional difficulties but also on the therapist's limitations, we also had to respect the privacy of the psychotherapy students. They had been open and frank in revealing themselves and the limits of their knowledge and experience in what was sometimes an uncomfortable exchange. So the people we have sitting around the seminar table are themselves composites, drawn from over forty professionals who attended the seminars in those six years and from students we have known elsewhere. Saul Wasserman is the only exception. He worked closely with me on some aspects of the chapter entitled "Punching Bags and Life-savers," reviewed and revised many drafts, and is identified as himself.

In discussing specific patients, we clustered together material from several cases with similar difficulties and created a composite case study from them. Many of the details we include do come from actual seminar cases, although some come from cases we have seen elsewhere. Any identifying material has been altered to guarantee anonymity. What is retained is a description of a clinical problem that numerous people suffer from, such as a boy who is too aggressive for his parents to manage, a young girl who has become anorexic, or an old man who is depressed, anxious, and frightened.

We have deviated from the actual seminars in another important way. In the sessions themselves, Bettelheim's was the predominant voice, and my participation was secondary to his. But in the writing and rewriting, it was I who did the greater share of the work. As a result, our discussions about how best to edit and present this material eventually led to a decision to split the seminar leader's role more equally between Bettelheim and myself, since that seemed to keep the flow of ideas moving in a more lively way and more accurately reflected the contributions each of us had made to the book in its final form. Since we shared so many ideas in common, we put words that he spoke on some occasions in my mouth, and some that I wrote or spoke are in his.

Some final editing aside, Bettelheim read and approved of as his most of the statements attributed to him in this book. When he became too debilitated to write, he dictated changes. We discussed the next-to-last draft just three weeks before his death, and we agreed about the direction that further revisions would take. After his death, I made changes along the lines we had agreed to, with the assistance he had arranged for of his longtime private editor, Joyce Jack, who had edited his last seven books.

However, in the final draft I found that I sometimes wished to include new material or substantially edit older material. Since Bettelheim would of course have no opportunity to review these latest changes, in making them I attributed to him only statements that were actual direct quotes from him, and all other new material to myself. This applies particularly to Chapter Four, which required substantial reediting. Overall, in my judgment, the viewpoint expressed in this book accurately represents Bruno Bettelheim's last position and views on psychotherapy, as well as my own, which he influenced so profoundly.

In teaching seminars I have conducted since the end of my collaboration with Bettelheim, I have been struck by how often I find the identical points covered by one or another chapter in this book arising spontaneously. This has encouraged me to think that the seminars in this book have a certain "prototypical" value and are therefore a useful teaching tool. The issues that are discussed come up repeatedly in psychotherapy, and I believe that the approach we advocate is as fresh and useful now as it was when the seminars transpired.

Psychotherapy is a highly individualistic field, whatever the therapist's theoretical beliefs. Each therapist tries on, adapts, and modifies other people's ideas or stances and weaves them together with his or her personal strengths and weaknesses to make this "impossible profession" his or her own. And today many different psychotherapies are being practiced with different techniques and goals. In no way does this book attempt to present a comprehensive approach to psychotherapy. Taken together, its chapters aim to give the reader a feeling for Bruno Bettelheim's approach to the patient and the stance he suggested a psychotherapist take if his goal was to help a patient "restructure his personality so he could live more comfortably with himself." I hope the book will give a feeling for the work a psychotherapist can do, from this psychoanalytic perspective.

Many participants in the seminar have remarked that they reflected on some comment Dr. B. made long after they heard it. I hope the reader will also experience the way Dr. B.'s comments stimulated critical thinking. At times, he made statements that I realized only after he had died would have benefited from elaboration. I have left some of those comments in the text so the reader can ponder them for him- or herself and wonder what else Bruno Bettelheim might have said had the discussion developed further.

I would like to thank the Spencer Foundation for giving us a grant that made the early stages of the project possible. The Rockefeller Foundation, Ms. Susan Garfield, the manager of its Bellagio Center Office, and Jo Ardovino, hostess at the Bellagio Center during our stay, deserve our thanks for their warm, gracious hospitality. And I would like to thank the Jewish Child Care Association of New York, which has given me the opportunity to continue working on this book while I served the agency and its children's needs.

Several individuals helped us prepare this material and bring it to its final form. I am grateful to Joyce Jack, both for her friendship and devotion to Bettelheim and for the substantial help she gave in bringing this manuscript to a form that was ready for submission. Over the time we worked together, I came to value her for herself as well as for her skills. Bruno Bettelheim's agent, Theron Raines, and mine, Jane Dystel, helped to bring this manuscript to Knopf's attention. And there I was in the wonderfully able hands of both Bobbie Bristol and Joan Keener, whose honesty, charm, skill, and forthrightness made for a second fruitful and enjoyable working relationship. I am very fortunate to have had this gift from Bettelheim, the opportunity to work with three talented editors.

Over the years, through every stage of this process, my dear friend, Peter Winn, helped with extensive suggestions and constant support. Another dear friend, one since childhood, Robert Kavet, also made numerous helpful comments. Alice Cooper, Claire Levine, and Karen Roekard helped with earlier drafts. Saul Wasserman helped us prepare the chapter that refers, in part, to his presentation. Since I differed with Bettelheim about autism's etiology, I wanted to consult an expert I knew well, respected, and could trust to be frank with me. I would like to thank Dr. Bryna Siegel of the University of California Medical Center in San Francisco for filling that role, helping me to understand the differences between Bettelheim's and the pseudonymous Dr. Daniel Berenson's points of view about autism and the difference between the autistic children whom Bettelheim treated at the Orthogenic School compared to children currently diagnosed as autistic. My colleagues and friends Drs. John Backman, David Port, John Stadler, and C. Barr Taylor made many helpful suggestions on the final manuscript. Helen Abrahamson gave devoted, superb secretarial help in this project's earliest stages; Margaret Forman gave the same much later on.

Many of the students who participated in the seminar were affected by it profoundly. As one told me on the phone just recently, "Not a day goes by in my life that I don't think of Bruno Bettelheim in my clinical work." I would like to thank several students by name who were particularly friendly to Bettelheim or me: Karen Axelsson, Neil Brast, Timmen Cermak, Mairin Doherty, Graehem Emslie, Peter Finkelstein, Miriam (Micki) Friedland, Peter Keefe, Kim Norman, Heather Ogilvie, and Alan Rapaport, and to thank the many others who attended these sessions for making the seminar so stimulating and for their part in making this book possible.

Lastly, I would like to thank my very patient family. My wife, Dorothy, has helped me throughout the many years it has taken to complete this project. And my wonderful children, Lisa Claire and Samuel Aaron, have all too often had a father whose attention was on the word processor instead of on them.

Before Bettelheim died, he and I drafted an introduction, and in it we discussed what our intentions were in this book: "We have tried to make a judicious selection from the enormous amount of material that emerged in these sessions. Of course, what this . . . volume presents is by no means an entire course in the teaching of psychoanalytic psychotherapy. But what we hope is that this small selection will give a feeling for what we tried to achieve and for a particular approach to the psychotherapy patient."

Alvin A Rosenfeld, M.D.

THE ART
OF THE
OBVIOUS

*Working with
Bruno Bettelheim:
A Personal View*

IN 1977, I BECAME Stanford University Medical School's new Director of Training in Child Psychiatry with a mandate to develop a first-rate program that prepared trainees to diagnose and treat disturbed children. I envisioned a program that integrated the richness of Stanford's psychiatric research with the psychodynamic approaches I had found so meaningful in my training and while on Harvard University Medical School's child-psychiatric faculty.

It was clear to me that in psychoanalytically oriented psychotherapy, psychiatrists in training would benefit from a teacher of advanced years, rich in the accumulated wisdom and experience that only a lifetime of practice, and reflection on practice, can provide. Thus, it seemed obvious that Bruno Bettelheim, who had retired to nearby Portola Valley in 1973, would be an excellent choice to help teach the psychodynamic approach. His numerous articles and books were well known; his intellectual achievements were legendary, and his commitment to a psychoanalytic perspective was unequivocal.

When Dr. B. (which is how he was widely known to colleagues and students) and I met in 1977, we discussed my background and plans for the program, and his desire to be more involved in teaching. I realized that on clinical matters and training issues we had a confluence of interests. He welcomed my warm invitation to teach a seminar, even though I had no money to pay him. For the three hours he donated weekly, his recompense was a fresh cup of coffee.

But my choosing Bettelheim was fraught with risk. He had a reputation for being difficult, indeed thorny. Furthermore, we had different views of America's role in Vietnam, an issue that had real, personal significance to each of us. From 1965 on, I had been strongly against our involvement, whereas Dr. B. had been widely quoted in the press as calling antiwar protesters "neo-Nazis" and blaming their parents for not teaching them "to fear." It was a painful war that set father against son, and anyone who took the view opposite to one's own, particularly one who voiced that view so strongly, seemed to be a natural enemy.

Dr. B. was a risky choice for another reason. His knowledge was not based on carefully designed experiments, but on many years of accumulated experience and his subjective understanding of children's and adults' inner lives. Although some very senior professors at the university and the Hoover Institute (a think tank located on the Stanford campus) respected Bettelheim deeply, the psychiatric faculty considered him "unscientific." They had made Bettelheim a visiting professor, but gave him little to do. Many psychiatric faculty members did not take kindly to his psychoanalytic orientation; others did not like Bettelheim's authoritative manner and willingness to express himself forcefully, particularly when he voiced profound doubts about the statistical and biochemical approaches that brought so much renown and research money to the department.

In our early conversations, however, I found Bettelheim had a useful perspective on my academic and intellectual interests. In the early 1970s, while I was affiliated with Harvard Medical School, I was among the group of researchers and clinicians who first identified and publicized the fact that prior sexual abuse in childhood was an important predisposing factor to psychiatric problems. With colleagues, I did studies and published papers that described approaches to and clinical interventions with patients who had been violated by incest and sexual abuse. I described the family context in which incest occurs and wrote a position paper on sexual abuse for the American Academy of Child Psychiatry that went to Congress and that the American Medical Association published in its main publication, the *Journal of the American Medical Association (JAMA)*.

My research continued after I came to Stanford. I published conceptual papers that explored the relationship between normal sexual development and overstimulation and incest in such publications as *The Journal of the American Academy of Child Psychiatry, The American Journal of Psychiatry*, and *JAMA*. Bettelheim prodded me to think more deeply about the findings my research group made in a large study I headed of sexual development in typical, well-to-do families and its connection to aberrant sexual development.

Bettelheim helped me even though he objected to the statistical approach I used in these studies. He admired science, but doubted whether methods useful in the physical sciences could measure and elucidate man's inner drives, needs, and passions. "All these scientific efforts are attempts to create certainty where Freud believed there was none . . . ," he said. "I believe that this basic contradiction is unbridgeable."

He spoke disparagingly of relying only on objective data: "This distrust of subjective approaches, including introspection, explains the physiological orientation of so much of American academic psychology. Physiology is measurable and quantifiable, while the right way for you to love someone is so difficult to find."

I once introduced Bettelheim to the late Robert Sears, a thoughtful developmental psychologist close to Bettelheim's age. Sears had pioneered the use of statistical methods in the study of child development. In their discussion, Sears said that the problem with current statistical efforts for studying children's emotional lives was that the researchers did not know how to "score affect," that is, to place a numerical value on what a person was feeling. Bettelheim disagreed. No person can measure another's feelings, he said. It is, he said, simply impossible to really know, let alone measure, what goes on inside another person. Not so, said Sears. Like other phenomena, emotions could be measured, but the job had to be done accurately. And there the polite line was drawn between these two sincere, thoughtful, brilliant men.

Dr. B. appealed to me for another reason that made some other faculty members leery of him. I had found a psychoanalytic perspective meaningful because it is a science *and* an art, possessing the intrinsic beauty and utility of both. Neither is an obviously superior way to know. Did Monet have a less valid understanding of color than people who can tell us about the spectral contents of hue?

I also wanted Bettelheim to help me further hone my own psychotherapeutic skills. I had reservations about how well I was communicating with a child I was treating, and felt that I was not making some crucial, yet very subtle, connection with the child. I told Bettelheim that I would like him to help me with my problems with this child. He said, "Let's try for a few weeks and see how it goes."

He was some teacher! In our discussions, he was able to put his finger on exactly the deficit I had been feeling. He pointed out ways for me to understand the child and to deepen the ongoing conversation that long-term psychotherapy is. Bettelheim would select some minuscule, seemingly unimportant detail that I just happened to mention, and helped me see that I recalled it because in this detail the child was telling me something crucial. He had an acute sense of what a specific patient needed at a particular moment. In our work during the first year we met, he occasionally suggested an intervention that seemed outrageous. The first time he did, I told him, "If I were Bruno Bettelheim, that might work. But I'm not." With quiet conviction, he said, "Just try it." I did what he suggested, and it worked. My relationship with the child deepened and improved.

Bettelheim taught me how to listen to children more carefully, to hear what they say, hypothesize what lies behind it, and communicate more precisely on the basis of both understanding and conjecture. He helped me to be less intellectual and more playful in the therapy I did. Years later he said to me, "It is hard for adults to learn to talk to children. Why? The only way to talk to children is to sink yourself into their position. But because our adult status is so recently acquired, we have to protect it at all costs." And another time someone asked him why we mythologize childhood as carefree and children as gentle souls. He replied, "We have this image of babyhood because we all want to have had one time where we had it so good. But it's an illusion. We never had it so good to begin with. . . . But there is another reason the [adult's] myth of childhood innocence dies very slowly. It is because of our own hostility in infancy, which we are trying to deny. It really has to do with being unable to accept all the hostile, aggressive thoughts we ourselves had in infancy, which prevents us from seeing it in children and protects our amnesia, so to say. . . ."

Although I came to love Dr. B. and to treasure our friendship, he was not an openly warm, affectionate, or physically demonstrative man. He usually called people by their professional names, and always retained a formal, proper demeanor in public. Except in his last two years, after two strokes, he was very private about his personal life. At times, he could be self-aggrandizing. But in his home, he treated everyone like an honored guest, with flawless graciousness and hospitality. Under the surface, I sensed a shy warmth and mischievousness which were reflected in the twinkle that often came to his eye and in the provocative brilliance of his casual comments.

Dr. B. had a wonderful sense of humor and sometimes, unpredictably, would share an anecdote from his childhood. A friend of mine was eager to have his wife stop breast-feeding their six-month-old child. To bolster his position, he asked Dr. B. to help him with this situation, expecting Dr. B. to be an apostle of strict child-rearing and to support him with stern psychoanalytic admonitions for his misguided wife. Dr. B. smiled. He said that when he had been born, his parents had gone to the Austrian provinces and hired a sixteen-year-old girl as his wet nurse. Everyone overlooked the fact that she had to have been a sexual delinquent at that age, and that she was necessarily leaving behind a child of her own. This nice girl, Dr. B. went on, a twinkle in his eye, had breast-fed him until he was four years old. Now, what exactly was the problem? My friend chose not to share this conversation with his wife.

Dr. B.'s brilliance was an odd gift, hard to describe. And it was brilliance in a field that has no universally agreed-upon guidelines, like the Table of Elements in chemistry. It is a field in which disagreements arise easily, even on basic assumptions. When Bettelheim taught about a clinical issue, he often raised questions that were difficult to answer. For those already established in the field, the confrontation with personal ignorance often was unsettling. For instance, Saul Wasserman headed a major child psychiatric inpatient unit when he discussed the case in Chapter Two. He recently said on rereading it, "It's hard to believe how dumb we were. I would handle that case so differently now."

It was easy to experience Bettelheim's questions as pestering or demeaning; after all, he knew what he was driving at. But he wanted you to figure it out for yourself. For example, Dr. B. might observe an attitude in you that you were unaware of, one that was impeding your capacity to empathize with the child you were treating. More often than not, you were behaving in a way that reflected some attitude your parents held which you had resented as a child but which you had had to accommodate to and internalize. So when Dr. B. shone a spotlight on that, you reacted with anger or defensiveness. Many participants in the seminar used that painful confrontation with themselves and their childhoods constructively. Several commented that what they had taken from this seminar and learned from Dr. B. had changed the direction of their lives or had influenced their professional careers profoundly.

Not everyone who came to the seminar felt that way. Because of my particular background and training, my own teaching style tends to be far less confrontational and more supportive than Bettelheim's was. He, in contrast, was the product of a rigorous, classical European education, and he had taught for many years at the University of Chicago, which was likewise famous for the rigor of its teaching methods. He could be very abrasive when disabusing a student of what he called "false assumptions" about psychoanalysis. (Less of this brusqueness may come through in the seminars presented here, since our purpose is not to give a biographical portrait but to represent our ideas as clearly as possible.) A number of students found Bettelheim's intensity and his aggressive style troubling, and stopped attending the seminars. Some of these people have since gone on to become excellent psychotherapists. Had they stayed, or had his teaching style been different, I am convinced that they would have gained a great deal and the seminar would have been enriched by their participation.

On one occasion, after a student had found Bettelheim's criticism particularly difficult to accept, several seminar members reproached him for insensitivity. In response, for the first and only time I heard him do so, Bettelheim explained his approach.

"When I teach psychoanalytic thinking, particularly on psychotherapy, I go out of my way to be difficult for the first few sessions, so that on the average fifteen to twenty percent of the students leave the class. I'm convinced that they are better off and that I am better off too. It entails considerable personal hardships to become a psychoanalyst, and you're better off not to go into the field if you can't deal with them. . . . The prime requirement for becoming a psychoanalyst is to undergo a personal analysis. In doing so, one experiences many times how very painful and upsetting a process it is, a personal experience that is absolutely necessary for later having empathy with the pains one's patient experiences when he or she is undergoing psychoanalysis.

"But since the majority of my students have not undergone psychoanalysis, they have to learn how upsetting the gaining of psychoanalytic insights can be for the individual. The sooner they learn that there will be disturbing experiences ahead for them, the better, so that if these early trials are too much for them, they can leave before too much damage is done to them. This is also the reason I have never taught required courses; I wanted to make it easy for my students to leave the class or seminar whenever they wanted.

"And that is why, before I agreed to Dr. Rosenfeld's request that we teach this seminar, I insisted that attendance be entirely voluntary, and that there would be no adverse repercussions whatsoever for any student who chose not to attend or who decided after a few sessions to drop out.

"Psychoanalysis simply isn't easy. It wasn't meant to be. Freud did not expect psychoanalysis to be for everybody. It helps only those who want it for themselves and who can take what the process and insights of psychoanalysis demand of an individual. Acceptance of psychoanalysis under false assumptions does psychoanalysis and the person involved no good. If someone doesn't want it, nothing benefits him or her more than getting out with the simultaneous opportunity to be angry at someone, in this case me. After such an experience, such a student will hold the view that it was my 'meanness' and not their own anxiety that made him leave. It is much better for such people to feel that they are rightly angry with me than to think that they could not take the pain inherent in psychoanalysis, or to think it is an easy process for anybody. Thus, in a deeper sense, what they experience as my 'meanness' is designed to protect them. And it works: They are angry at me, and I can take their anger without thinking any less of them."

The experience in the seminar was very different if you recognized that when you presented, Bettelheim's questions were designed to get you to think about something important, so you could discover it for yourself, to become aware of an attitude that made you less effective as a therapist. Then your experience was anxiety-provoking *and* productive. If you struggled to comprehend what he was showing you about yourself, you realized that your intense reaction confirmed that he had touched on something important. And then you struggled harder. "I can't teach you to do psychotherapy," I remember Dr. B. saying. "Only you can do that. I can only teach you how to think about psychotherapy."

"Psychoanalysis is the art of the obvious," Dr. B. often said. And, as you worked your way through the problems of a particular case, as you stripped away blinders you had worn since childhood, blinders that stopped you from seeing what would have been clear to you as a child, you would grasp what Dr. B. was saying. Soon, you could no longer remember a time when you did not see it. The insight seemed to be so clear, so much your own, something you had seen and known all along. Wasn't it?

Like the good psychoanalyst who helps you make discoveries on your own, Dr. B. made the insights yours. "Self-discovery is tremendously valuable to the person who discovers himself," he said in one seminar. "To be discovered by somebody else has never done any good to anybody. You know, there's the story that when Columbus discovered America, the Indians said, 'We are discovered. That is the end of us.' And indeed it was. That is why the psychoanalytic situation was created to promote *self*-discovery."

Over time, it became hard to know where your ideas began and Dr. B.'s left off. Interacting with Bettelheim actually changed the way you saw the world and thought about people. For some, his profound influence was a source of resentment, which made it easier to focus on what was difficult about his personality than to admit a humbling debt. When I wrote papers using ideas of Bettelheim's that I had incorporated into my own understanding and outlook, I asked him whether he wished me to give him credit. His answer was that he had simply shared ideas with me, and they belonged to everyone. I never heard him take any other position.

He was an expert who talked common and uncommon sense, and whose insights and ideas had utility in my clinical work and personal life. He could discuss a theoretical issue, or how to select a nanny, or why my daughter sang before she spoke. Sometimes merely by shifting my perspective on a seemingly insoluble paradox just one or two degrees from where I was focused, he showed me a narrow corridor through which I could see clearly to the other side. Many of us who worked with him through the years had that experience, and termed it his "genius." But to this sort of acclamation, Dr. B. answered something like: "You gave me all the information. You knew it too. But you spoke so quickly, you didn't listen to yourself."

Though he had worked hard and was proud to have achieved fame, he realized it was of limited importance, especially when his wife was still alive. "Sure it's nice to have your work recognized and quoted. But in another way it doesn't mean much at all. The people you really care about and hope will care about you don't give a hoot about what you write. They form their opinions by how you treat them. And giving talks takes an old man like me away from home and my wife. So it's a mixed bag, you see. My time is precious. It's all I have left."

BRUNO BETTELHEIM's life had gone through many twists before he had arrived in California. He was born in Vienna in 1903, into an affluent, assimilated Jewish family. He studied art history and aesthetics at the University in Vienna and, at age twenty-three, went into his family's lumber business when his father died. He never felt that he was much of a businessman and longed for a more scholarly life. He became involved with the psychoanalytic movement when it was still something of a frontier enterprise and, although still a businessman in Vienna, went into personal psychoanalysis with Richard Sterba. His first wife, Gina Weinmann, participated in Anna Freud's early experimental efforts to treat children psychoanalytically. She took a deeply disturbed child Anna Freud had referred into the Bettelheim home to live with them. This was Bettelheim's first experience with an autistic child. The syndrome had not yet been named.

Bettelheim considered himself a member of the "third generation" of psychoanalysts. He was eight years younger than Anna Freud, whom he became acquainted with through his wife, and he knew many others directly involved with the relatively early development of psychoanalysis and especially child psychoanalysis.

In one of the Stanford seminars, a participant challenged Dr. B. for relying so heavily on Sigmund Freud's teachings. "The researchers you criticize for disregarding subjective experience and behavior's meaning at least have valid data I can evaluate and replicate. That's the problem with psycho-analysis. It seems to me to have become a brand of religion that depends on the true believers' perceptions."

"The fact that psychoanalysis has not been validated em-pirically does not make it a religion," Dr. B. replied. "Mind you, I have no aversion to religion per se. I always ask what the price of this religion is and what are its benefits. If I have to dwell in hell for an eternity, the price of believing in sal-vation seems too high. Not to mention that I have to sacrifice the one life I have for the hope of being saved.

"I've lived through too many religions which proved false. When I was a young boy in school, the unsplittable atom was the prevalent religion of science, an absolute we could count on. Now physicists have discovered more subatomic particles than anybody can figure out." He paused and pondered for a moment. "Maybe we were better off when the atom was not splittable. . . .

"I personally am committed to psychoanalysis because it has provided me with the most acceptable and useful image of man, as well as with methods for helping people. But by 'methods for helping people,' I do not necessarily mean to analyze them. You certainly cannot analyze little children, because young children do not have a high ability to intro-spect.

"Classical analysis requires what Freud or some of his fol-lowers talked about as the splitting of the ego into one that observes and one that experiences. And my God, kids have enough trouble just developing an ego. To expect them to split it is ridiculous. So what we do is provide the child with experiences which we hope are constructive and are based on our psychoanalytic understanding of man and of human development.

"If child analysis had not been invented by his daughter, Sigmund Freud never would have accepted it. Too many parameters are necessary. Even Anna Freud said that she would never treat a child whose parents, or at least whose mother, had not been analyzed. This is exactly contrary to the method her father developed. In adult psychoanalysis, the rest of the family is kept entirely outside of the experience. But in child analysis, you have to manipulate the environment at least in part. We provide the children with special schools . . . we try to arrange for better living conditions, which certainly is not introspection. But these arrangements are based on a psychoanalytic understanding of man and his needs."

Notwithstanding Dr. B.'s commitment to psychoanalysis, he appreciated that Sigmund Freud's own thinking had evolved and changed over the course of his long career. "One doesn't write more than twenty volumes and remain the same person over time and over this experience. If you read Freud's last finished work, *Moses and Monotheism*, which is a fantasy, a glorious fantasy but still a fantasy, it is an entirely different Freud from the author of the seventh chapter of *The Interpretation of Dreams*."

Bettelheim also anticipated that psychoanalysis would change after Anna Freud died in 1982. "Even though the psychoanalytic treatment model has undergone, and I think probably will undergo, continuous change, what will remain through all the changes is an image of man, particularly the importance of the unconscious, and such facts as repression and the various other defense mechanisms. These add a dimension to our image of man that was not available before Freud, an image based strictly on introspection."

Bettelheim had strong feelings about the contrast between psychoanalysis and methods that aimed to change people's behavior without understanding their inner lives. "Behaviorism holds that man's essence can be readily changed, that man can be made to function as efficiently as a well-oiled machine," Dr. B. said. "In contrast, although Freud believed that some aspects of man could be changed somewhat, others were intractable because they arose out of man's very nature. . . .

"Psychoanalysis focuses on a person's inner life, on wishes, fantasies, conflicts and the contradictions in the personality. Psychoanalysis tries to distinguish between those that are consequences of our life experiences and those that are unavoidable aspects of our nature. But to understand an individual's inner life, the complexity of human *feelings*, including 'love,' must be appreciated.

"I am saying something that is disturbing to those who believe that man is infinitely perfectible. Love includes our destructive tendencies, which are engaged in a constant battle with our life [or constructive] drives. Freud conceptualized this tension as the conflict between Thanatos and Eros."

From 1938 to 1939, Bettelheim was incarcerated in two concentration camps, Dachau and Buchenwald. Throughout the rest of his life, memories from that year haunted him. He told me that he often had nightmares about the camps. Yet he wove what he observed and experienced there into his understanding of people. Out of this, he built a remarkable practice and career.

We were once talking about how one survives severe maltreatment. I was exploring that psychological phenomenon in a novel I was writing about grief and recovery. Bettelheim replied: "Up to a point you can resist. But if you let yourself be beaten down psychologically, economically, and morally, you no longer can *believe* that you can resist or escape. . . . Even a prison is a different place if you say, 'Here I am and I can't get out,' or if you sit in prison and spend all day plotting your escape. . . . It's an inner attitude. Every chance where you could do something that you didn't is a demonstration to you that you can't do it. Every chance you use, even if you don't succeed, might give you the hope the next time you'll succeed."

The New York family whose autistic child had lived in the Bettelheims' Vienna home was politically well connected. In 1939, they persuaded Governor Lehman of New York and Eleanor Roosevelt to intercede with the Nazis on Bruno Bettelheim's behalf.

Eventually, Dr. B. came to the United States nearly destitute. As he told it to me, soon thereafter, he and his first wife were divorced. He wrote to Trude Weinfeld, who had worked in Anna Freud's school and had fled to Australia, and she joined him in Chicago, where they married. Bettelheim taught at a women's college in Rockford, Illinois. In addition, he participated in an eight-year study to evaluate art education funded by the Rockefeller Foundation at the University of Chicago. In 1944, top administrators at the University of Chicago asked him to take over as head of the Sonia Shankman Orthogenic School, an institution for severely disturbed and psychotic children. There he taught psychoanalytic psychotherapy to the school's staff, and, at first in collaboration with Emmy Sylvester, he innovated and refined "milieu therapy," the method he found most productive in treating the school's extremely disturbed children. Milieu therapy requires that all facets of the child's life—the physical environment and all the people the child lives with, as well as the therapy sessions—be considered aspects of the curative process. Thus, Bettelheim met with housekeepers, counselors, teachers, and concerned himself with every detail of the Orthogenic School's daily functioning, design, and physical plant. Bettelheim habitually spent sixteen and eighteen hours a day at the school, making certain that it ran as he thought it should.

The Orthogenic School became famous for its therapeutic work with the small percentage of its students who were autistic. But most of its children were seriously disturbed in other ways, and it helped a great many of them as well. Bettelheim's experience was drawn from treating many different types of children, but his best known writings were about the treatment of very disturbed, psychotic children. Yet his ideas have direct application in understanding and treating the severely abused and neglected children who interest many clinicians today, including me.

In the years after he came to the United States, Bettelheim served as an educator and healer. Through lectures, books, and articles, he became known internationally for his contributions to our psychoanalytic understanding of severely disturbed children, of the concentration camp experience and the Holocaust, and of artistic creativity. He published for both professional and lay audiences; his wisdom and humanity were appreciated widely. Through his teaching and writing, Dr. B. moved and inspired many students, colleagues, and readers on a profound level. His views were forceful, clear, usually unequivocal, often provocative. He was no stranger to criticism and often was embroiled in heated controversy, whether about the cause of autism, about whether Anne Frank's family might have spent their time in hiding more constructively planning an escape, or about the anti–Vietnam War movement. Even when one disagreed vehemently with him (and many people did), his point of view was so well thought out and compelling that it caused one to think more deeply. By arguing with him, one came to understand one's own position more fully.

When Dr. B. finally retired at seventy, his heart was weak, his circulation poor. He needed a place to live with a more congenial climate than Chicago's, and less hazardous than its icy streets are in winter. Some of the Bettelheims' Viennese and Chicago friends had retired to the San Francisco Bay area, where the Bettelheims had spent a productive year in the early 1970s when Dr. B. was a guest at Stanford's Center for the Advanced Study of the Behavioral Sciences. So in 1973, they moved to California, where Bettelheim became a visiting professor at Stanford University and hoped to teach there in his accustomed way.

In seventeen years of retirement, he published numerous essays and books, among them: *The Uses of Enchantment*, which won the National Book Award, *On Learning to Read* with Karen Zelan, *Freud and Man's Soul*, *A Good Enough Parent*, and *Freud's Vienna*.

Once when Bettelheim was talking about a patient in psychoanalysis, he said, "After all, that is what you need an analyst for, to give you the courage to do what you are afraid to do alone." When I mentioned that the analyst he was describing sounded like the Wizard of Oz, Dr. B. agreed. "In this whole story, my favorite character is the Cowardly Lion. I'm a coward too, you know. And that always has stood me in excellent stead." I noted that his reputation was quite different. "Well," Bettelheim replied with candor, "if you are a cowardly lion, you must roar loudly." In Dr. B.'s life, he told me, it was his wife, Trude, to whom he was deeply devoted, who had given him the courage to attempt to succeed in America.

Dr. B. had not been in good health since his fifties, and Trude was about nine years his junior. They had always expected, therefore, that he would predecease her and had planned accordingly. He was never the same after she died in October 1984, following a prolonged bout with cancer. Not long thereafter, Dr. B. moved to Santa Monica, California.

Despite Dr. B.'s deep depression and his sense that he was alone without her, he did endure, living and working creatively. Then, in 1988, came the first of two strokes that made writing hard and the chores of everyday life even more difficult for him. For the last two years of his life, from 1988 until 1990, all who knew him well could attest that Bruno Bettelheim was a deeply depressed and exhausted man. He had a disorder of the esophagus that made swallowing very difficult, so that he could eat only pureed foods. He lost considerable weight. But even then, despite his advanced age, he agreed to esophageal surgery. The surgery went well, and he felt better as he once again could enjoy a more varied diet. But he was preyed on by that fear that haunts many elderly people who have been strong-willed and independent, that another stroke would leave him helpless.

Each time I flew to California to visit him, I found him more debilitated. He felt that his body had abandoned him completely, but, he added, "unfortunately, my mind has been left behind." He was thin and needed a cane to walk. Each time I visited, our walks were shorter and slower even though he was making a great effort. Near the end, he was unable to drive. He could write only with great effort; his once-flowing handwriting, with its large bold curves, became small and cramped. He needed a constant companion to help him, including bathing him, which was difficult for a proud, formal, shy, and very private man. The feeling of helplessness was a particular affront to the sense of dignity, integrity, autonomy, and self-control that Dr. B. valued. Near the end he once said to me, "Thanatos has won out. I have no interest in life anymore."

Many people have said that reading what Dr. B. wrote about surviving under extreme conditions sustained them emotionally through their darkest times. That may be why so many, including patients in whom he had tried to inspire survival, felt betrayed when he took his own life in March 1990.

Dr. B. had not given up quickly or easily. He lost his desire to live when his wife died, a feeling that became intense and insistent from March 1988 on, when he had the first stroke. Yet in the next two years he tried all available remedies that neurologists or psychiatrists recommended, including physical rehabilitation, reentering psychoanalysis, and taking numerous antidepressant, stimulant, antipanic, and other medications. He tried to become more active in teaching. He was never abandoned by friends, old or new. When I visited him in Washington a few weeks before he died, the phone rang at least every half hour. But in his desolation, Dr. B. maintained that no one ever called. When I pointed out the contradiction, he conceded that I was right, but said he still felt forlorn. I can only wonder whether the strokes also had caused some circumscribed neurologic impairment in his short-term memory.

At age eighty-six, Dr. B. knew he did not have another ten years of good life ahead of him. The only questions were how soon he would die, whether he would first have to suffer further humiliating debility, and whether he should take matters into his own hands. His role model was Sigmund Freud, who, when he was eighty-three and suffering intolerably from a sixteen-year-long battle with cancer, had his physician, Max Schur, give him an overdose of morphine. But suicide was looked upon differently by the Viennese of Freud's and Bettelheim's time. (In fact, a year or two before Dr. B. ended his life, his sister, who was his only sibling, committed suicide in New York City.) In his last two years, Dr. B. repeatedly asked physician friends to assure him that if he were *totally* incapacitated and unable to commit suicide, they would help him out of his misery with a morphine injection. If someone would promise him that, he said from time to time, he would give up his talk of suicide. Unfortunately, no one could take the risk of helping him. When he decided that suicide was his only solution, he wanted his act to be private. So he tried to arrange a trip to Holland, where, he told me, suicide is tolerated, although not legal. He did not want any kind of public spectacle, but he also knew that although others might see him as a symbol, he was a real person who was living in agony every day.

I guess each of us has to decide whether we have the right to make such a choice. He consulted the Hemlock Society and followed their advice exactly. Bruno Bettelheim always had great respect for expert advice.

WHILE THIS BOOK has been in process, a certain amount of highly critical material centering on Bettelheim's personality—complex, perfectionistic, and demanding—has been published. Bettelheim had a long and distinguished career, a disposition to speak out on many controversial topics, and a reputation for keenness of mind and willingness to join in intellectual combat. His goal was to understand clearly and deeply, not to be best-liked.

Dr. B.—as already noted at some length—could be abrasive; everyone who knew him felt this personally at one time or another. Also, everyone who knew him had strong feelings about him, so it is not surprising that critical things were said about him while he was alive and after he died. What is surprising is that defamatory articles about him, whether true or not, appeared and were widely reported only after he died. I became a friend after his retirement, so I am in no position to comment on stories about what Bettelheim did or did not do at the Orthogenic School. In August 1990, four months after Dr. B. died, a reporter from a major national magazine called me for information about the accusations against Dr. B. I asked her why these criticisms were first coming up when he was no longer able to defend or explain himself. With some reluctance, she replied, "Because an estate can't sue for libel."

Many students I called to tell that this book was nearing completion expressed their deep gratitude to Dr. B. One said he had become a psychoanalyst because his experiences in the seminar had opened his eyes to man's inner life. Another said, "Be sure to tell them how blind I was. It took Dr. B. to show me that." Dr. B. was a flame who in his life lit many other candles; some he knew, others knew him through his writings. These were lives that were permanently changed for the better because they had the good fortune to interact with Bruno Bettelheim and his remarkably clear and perceptive mind. For myself, with the sadness that goes with finally saying good-bye to a beloved friend, colleague and mentor, I would like to pay tribute to him, with words attributed to Sigmund Freud: "The voice of reason is soft, but insistent."

Alvin A Rosenfeld, M.D.

The First Encounter

ONE MIGHT THINK that starting the first psychotherapy session with a new patient ought to be simple. You just say hello and you're off. But the first session is so much more: It is a critical moment that can determine the course of years of therapy. Therefore, in our seminar series, Bruno Bettelheim and I devoted at least one session every year to discussing how to greet a new patient. Dr. B. often said, "The end is in the beginning," meaning that the way one enters a relationship with a patient sets the stage for much that follows, perhaps even the final outcome.

Dr. B. compared the way Sigmund Freud established a proper atmosphere for psychoanalytic sessions to a play's brilliantly realized stage design, one that conveys a vivid feeling for the drama about to be enacted. On Freud's psychoanalytic stage, a couch is the dominant prop. It conveys important, subliminal messages to a patient before any words are spoken. The couch makes it clear that patient and analyst are beginning a relationship that differs from all other relationships. By asking the patient to lie down, Freud was suggesting that relaxation was desirable and hinting that regression, so frowned upon in other areas of life, was invited and accepted. Furthermore, since we usually are supine in bed when dreaming, the presence of the couch intimates that dreams play a very important role in the analytic setting.

By placing the analyst on a chair behind the patient, Freud put the patient at center stage. The analyst, sitting behind the patient, will concentrate on what the patient's words tell him and on what the patient's actions reveal.

Our seminar's setting was far less carefully orchestrated. Every Tuesday at 1:30 P.M., we gathered around the polished conference room table in the Children's Hospital at Stanford's outpatient psychiatry department. Dr. B. sat at the table's head and I sat at his left. On such a Tuesday in the summer of 1983, Dr. B. introduced himself to two trainees who were at the seminar for the first time, Renee Kurtz, an advanced social work student, and Jason Winn, a new child psychiatry resident. The others were seminar "regulars." Michael Simpson was a child psychiatrist who had finished his training and now was in private practice in nearby Menlo Park. He had attended the seminar for years, coming as often as he could despite his busy practice. Gina Andretti, a child psychologist from Milan, Italy, who was spending two years in advanced training at Stanford, and Bill Sanberg, a clinical psychologist who usually worked with adults, had been coming to the seminar for just over a year. He had grown up in a Washington suburb, had gotten his Ph.D. from a famous Southern university and had held a post-doctoral fellowship in one of the Stanford programs. Sandy Salauri, a clinical social worker in Stanford University psychiatry department's outpatient clinic, had been attending the seminar for just over six months.

Dr. B. was known as a challenging teacher. When he looked around the table, students sometimes averted their eyes so that Dr. B. would not call upon them and ask if they had a case to present. Today, however, I was surprised to see that, in her first seminar session, Renee seemed eager to attract his attention.

Renee had grown up in Los Angeles before moving north to go to college and social work school at Berkeley. Though outwardly deferential, she possessed spunk, inquisitiveness, and intellectual keenness. She waited in the brief silence and then spoke. "I really need help. I'm supposed to see my first child case tomorrow. I want to understand him better before I see him, but I know only a few facts from his chart. He's seven years old, his name is Simeon, and he sets fires."

"I wonder if you already know too much," Dr. B. said. "You speak of the boy's chart as containing 'facts.' But you ought to regard the whole record as hearsay."

"But it's not hearsay," Renee protested. "Senior clinicians prepared that chart."

"And I'm sure they prepared what they considered to be an accurate record," Dr. B. said. "However, it tells you only how they interpreted the boy's words and actions, their emphases and omissions. But for you these observations are a hindrance."

Renee looked uncertain, so I offered an amplification on Dr. B.'s point. "The chart shows you details that other people wanted to draw your attention to. And since these people are smart and experienced and you want to learn, you ultimately will gain from what they saw. But now is not the right time. In your own first encounter with the patient you will perceive far more than you can possibly register consciously. How does this boy look? How is he dressed? Do his clothes look like ones he's selected himself? How does he walk? Has he brought along a special toy? If so, what is it? How is he holding or playing with it? Does he play with the toys in your playroom or simply look at them? Is he interacting with his parents in the waiting room, or is he playing alone in the corner? Does he look at you when you introduce yourself?

What seems to interest him in you or in the playroom? How does he speak or even refuse to speak to you? After all, people can be silent in as many different ways as they can speak openly. Out of all these initial conscious and subliminal observations, with your own sense of the situation, you will select what to focus on in your first meeting.

"What you learn about a person in advance influences what you observe and react to. When you are a beginning therapist and are nervous about your first encounter, you will be likely to screen your perceptions to select the ones that struck your teachers. But because you will be looking to confirm what your role models have noticed, you may overlook crucial details that no one has ever seen before."

Renee looked perplexed. "Why can't I pay attention to my perceptions but also read the record to help me see more?"

"You can," I answered. "Just not yet. The details you'll see tomorrow are unique because they emerge from what you evoke from the patient, part of how he chooses to present himself to *this* therapist, you, on *this* day, and are part of his reaction to you as a person and therapist. If you read the chart, you may be tempted to look for what others noticed. So the new patient won't see a unique, genuine Renee Kurtz, responding spontaneously to what strikes her. He will see a woman trying to be a good student in her teacher's eyes. From the beginning, you will have introduced an artificiality into what has to be an intensely personal relationship—and both of you will feel the strain.

"Furthermore, like most children his age, he may believe that all adults are in cahoots. And he knows he's being brought because, supposedly, he set a fire. So in a first session with you, at best, he expects that you will judge him. At worst, he may view his first session with you as part of the punishment his parents and school have threatened him with.

"But if he senses that you have no prior knowledge about him, there's a slim chance he'll believe you are embarking on a mutual journey of discovery. And at least about the topic of who he is and why he does what he does, he is as much of an authority as you and possesses far more pertinent facts. He will sense your alertness, curiosity, and humility and will respond to these, often in a positive fashion. And that will give psychotherapy a chance of starting more fruitfully."

"When I was at the Orthogenic School," Dr. B. said, "we frequently had a potential patient described to us as 'a perfect terror, uncontrollable and vicious.' Yet when I would finally meet this 'monster,' he would turn out to be a terrified little child. But despite my having experienced this so often, each time it happened I could not free myself entirely from wondering when and how the child would explode. I am sure that somehow the child sensed that. If this was true for me, and I had hundreds of such experiences, it must be even truer for a beginner.

"Another factor comes into play. I am well aware that we all have anxieties when we start with a new patient. But because of the information you have, your anxiety is much more under your control than the patient's, and he is not insensitive to this imbalance. Not only that, you know and he knows that you know something about him, but he doesn't know what. And he knows nothing about you personally. This imbalance skews the relationship.

"Even the most experienced psychoanalysts have a problem with this issue of superiority," Dr. B. went on. "Although I can't prove it, I suspect that part of the traditional rule of silence, or relative silence, really came about because some early analysts realized how difficult it is not to play superior; our training and knowledge tempt us to feel that way. But this attitude is the most destructive thing for the patient."

"Well, my problem is not superiority. It's inexperience," Renee replied. "I'm sure that just because I'm a beginner, I will completely miss the significance of a great deal in each session. It doesn't seem fair to this young boy or his parents to take months to learn things I simply could have read in his chart before starting."

"Let me tell you an anecdote about Freud," Dr. B. said. "Shortly after Rorschach developed his inkblot test as a way to explore patients' imaginations, a psychologist brought news of it to Vienna. Some younger analysts, perhaps like you wishing to work more quickly, were taken with the test and persuaded Freud to have it demonstrated to him.

"Freud was duly impressed with what one could discover from an individual's associations to inkblots. Naturally, some of those present expected him to find the test useful in his work. But when Freud was asked whether he thought it might be of value to the practicing analyst, his reply was a curt 'No.' He explained that if he knew what the Rorschach test would reveal before he got to know a patient, he no longer would be able to analyze the patient well. His knowledge would interfere with his curiosity about what made the patient tick.

"Freud considered the analyst's curiosity to be the energizer in psychoanalysis, what kept the analysis from becoming stale or rote. Freud's wish to discover things he did not know about the patient was as important in this long process as the patient's wish to make himself understood.

"For example, consider what would happen to your own relationship with a patient who has known you for a long time and finally feels safe and trusting enough to share a deep secret. He gives you the secret as a gift or sign of growing trust. If, when he does, your inner reaction is 'That's old news to me. What took you so long to tell me?'—something, by the way, you might feel but would never say—might not the patient have a strong reaction to your lack of excitement? Might he ask himself why he should take the trouble to continue his self-exploration and to explain himself to somebody who already seems to know it all? But if the patient does not explain himself to the therapist, he will fail to explain himself to himself. And explaining yourself to yourself is fundamental to psychotherapy's being effective.

"When a person discovers things about himself he had not known before, he may also find out why he has failed to know these things, why he has repressed them and how he wishes to act differently in the future.

"If we have no advance information about our patient, instead of reacting 'That's old stuff' to his discovery, which is his 'gift' to us, we will be inwardly excited. Whether or not we say something, the patient senses our reaction and is stimulated to do even better. His negative view of himself will be challenged. He will begin to see himself as someone valuable who can provide insights and facts that the therapist, a person he considers valuable, finds interesting and worthwhile. He will want to provide more. He becomes eager to go on with therapy, and we therapists enjoy our new-found knowledge and ability to understand. Therefore, we look forward to the next session almost as much as he does."

At this point I interjected: "If I were you, Renee, I would look at the record after seeing the patient for the first or, probably better, the second session, because I feel that this early in your training you should learn from what experienced people have said. By waiting until then, you'll have your own perceptions to compare to what's in the record. But you should also keep in mind that as you become more experienced, you can gain a great deal if you wait much longer before you read the record. In the time that you'll be working blind to the 'facts' in the record, before the patient himself shares them with you in his own way and from his own point of view, you and he will be forging a relationship of mutual appreciation. When you finally do learn the information, you will understand it in the framework of that relationship. In this unique context, you may be far less judgmental than the record or some evaluator who saw the patient only once or twice."

"That's why clinical education has a long tradition of training in observational skills," Dr. B. said. "If one develops one's own observational skills and learns to let patients talk about themselves, one can learn an enormous amount just by listening and observing. Professor Wolf, a Gestalt psychologist, had people walk into the lecture room and across the podium with a sack covering their heads and most of their bodies, so that one could see only their feet. From observing how they walked, Wolf was able to describe their personalities. He could have focused on their handwriting, as graphologists do, the way they spoke, or how they performed any other characteristic act. If one concentrates on one particular feature and learns to pay careful attention to it in every encounter, over time one may in fact learn how this feature expresses personality. Of course, one must watch at least fifty or sixty people walk before beginning to appreciate what the differences signify. After you learn what one aspect of behavior tells you about a person, you may concentrate on a second and then on a third, and in this fashion you will develop your own skill in seeing what the minute differences among people's behavior say about them."

"Hearing about what Professor Wolf could do makes me feel even more so that I need guidance," Renee said.

"When Professor Wolf demonstrated his observational skill with people wearing sacks over their heads, he was not practicing psychotherapy," I said. "He was making a virtuoso diagnostic performance, rather like a brilliant analysis of a Rorschach test. We all can make it a lifetime goal to increase our alertness to every nuance of a patient's movements and expressions, to deepen our understanding of how a patient reveals his feelings and personality. And that might help if you want to do quick personality assessments for some particular purpose. But healing takes place in psychotherapy only when we place our observational skills at the service of the relationship between us and the patient.

"Renee, you are beginning your career. You're bright and obviously eager to learn. Of course you feel you need guidance. I would be very worried if someone beginning this 'impossible profession' already felt thoroughly confident. I hope you'll find guidance at this seminar. But no matter what you learn from us, your patients will be your best teachers.

"Furthermore, each of you has at least twenty-five years of experience in observing people and interpreting what you've seen. However, much that you observe and many judgments you make take place on an unconscious level rather than being organized for therapeutic purposes. We will help you to make the knowledge of human behavior you have already accumulated more explicit so that you can use it consciously.

"That was how I learned. In my first weeks of psychiatric training, I sat in a conference room with the twenty-four other new psychiatric residents. An instructor brought a slender, vivacious young woman into the classroom. He said hello to her and explained that in about an hour he would to speak to her at length. Their entire interaction lasted a minute or less and then she left.

"We spent the next hour discussing the patient, describing what we had seen and heard, speculating about her life, and hypothesizing about what might be troubling her. Then the instructor asked the girl to return and interviewed her for half an hour. We residents were amazed to find out how much we had observed in that first minute. We learned that we had correctly deduced not just that she was anorexic (long before all the professional and media attention paid to eating disorders) but also details about the sports she played, how she related to friends, family, and schoolwork, and why she dressed as she did.

"I doubt that any of us could have come to our conclusions alone. We all saw the same behaviors and heard the same few responses, but the discussion shaped our thinking and made our intuitions conscious. With the instructor's guidance, we learned from each other.

"That's one way we develop as clinicians. We often speak of the first encounter because the first time you see a new patient, you will observe and hear things that you may not see again for years. Over time, you learn to make careful observations at that first meeting. Sometimes what stands out is some seemingly minor detail that you keep seeing in your mind's eye but cannot figure out why. Because it has struck you deeply and subliminally, you know it's very important. Over time, you come to understand what it means and why the patient chose, perhaps unconsciously, to show it to you during your first encounter.

"When you're starting out, it's very hard to simply see and concentrate on what's there. You're nervous and want something to grab onto so your anxiety will be diminished. That's often what you use the record for, to put a child's behavior into some clearly defined category so you feel anchored. You see a child play with a mother, a father, and a child doll and say to yourself, 'Aha. That must reflect the oedipal issue, which his evaluation said he was struggling with,' and you feel less at sea. I did the same thing. It wasn't constructive. Still, only after I had seen enough patients could I make the field my own, feeling secure enough to use my own perceptions as my compass. Until then, I had neither the courage nor the resources to do it. So I'm not surprised that you are struggling with it."

Dr. B. disagreed. "Even if that is the case, you are far more likely to build up your inner resources by being forced to do so than by being told that doing so is to your advantage." He spoke directly to Renee. "Tomorrow, as a beginner, you will miss many clues to this young boy's personality. But not all of them. Your most urgent task is not to build a mental construct of his personality. It is to help him realize that you care about what he is feeling and how he sees you.

"But in the long run, to be a successful child therapist, you need a great deal of experience with what is more or less normal behavior. So in the next years, spend time with and observe children. You are not really going to understand pathology unless you first ask yourself what is the reasonable, 'expectable' reaction for a parent or child of some particular age. If you observe enough 'normal' mothers and children, deviant reactions will stand out as such. But it takes time to learn this."

Dr. B. glanced at a familiar textbook on child psychotherapy that Renee had in front of her. "That book says that the first psychotherapy interview can be a tense time for any child. That statement only speaks about one part of a relationship. It never says that meeting a new patient is tense for the psychotherapist too. In this way, this author takes the therapist out of the situation."

"He takes the therapist out of the entire equation as if what happens isn't an interaction," I said. "What is important in preparing to see this boy for the first time tomorrow is that you have thought about you and the patient as a twosome and of therapy as a shared adventure. In this way you establish that the two of you will develop some kind of bond. If you think of your *relationship* with this new individual, you won't feel entirely at a loss about how to behave. Even if your preparations turn out to be deficient, the fact that you have tried to be prepared helps protect you from having anxiety debilitate you. Of course, you can't get too attached to your plan, even though you spent time developing it.

"Let's say that on actually meeting this new patient you realize that he is entirely different from what you had anticipated. Or let's say that over time you learn that your initial reactions were 'wrong.' You then might wonder how and why you had been in error, what the mistake teaches you about yourself, your foibles, presumptions, and prejudices, and how in future cases, you might better control whatever it is in you that had led you astray in this situation."

"I can illustrate the centrality of this concern with two case examples from the patients' points of view," Dr. B. said. "In the first, a woman, on first meeting her female therapist, received the strong impression that the therapist acted not like a doctor, but like a businesswoman: objective in manner and more interested in getting her fee than in helping the patient. But the therapist's reputation overawed the patient, and being a very insecure person, she did not dare say what she felt or feel free to consult another therapist.

"For many months this woman continued to see the therapist regularly, never able to tell her what her first impression had been. The treatment went nowhere, and the patient finally ended it after more than a year. Not only did she derive no benefit from the money, time, and energy she had spent with this therapist but she also was so dejected that, for several years, she did not attempt to receive the treatment she badly needed.

"The second patient, a man in his late forties, on first meeting his therapist, was very disappointed that the therapist was a man much younger than himself. The patient had hoped and expected his therapist to be much older and more mature than he himself was. Again, the patient did not dare to tell his therapist about this disappointment. Fortunately, this therapist sensed that he was not what the patient had expected, so he asked the patient right away how he felt about having a therapist younger than he was. Since the therapist had so correctly gauged what was going on in the patient's mind, this patient's confidence in the therapist's competence was restored, and then all went well.

"If the second therapist had *not* considered the patient's reaction to him and the therapeutic situation the most urgent order of business, he probably would have spent that first session looking for clues to major events and patterns of behavior, which he may have heard about from the referring internist. Then the patient would have responded in the way he thought he was supposed to act in this new situation. But the therapist showed the patient how important and valid he considered the patient's point of view. In this way, the therapist enabled the patient to perceive him as a genuine person with whom, therefore, he could be his genuine self.

"The therapist can't always correctly gauge why the patient is uncomfortable or angry with him. But working this way, even your mistakes will be your own, not someone else's. If you didn't make mistakes, you might frighten patients with your seeming omniscience. Because the one who always has to be right is the patient. In some ways, psychotherapy is a power relationship. The patient has the power and always is right. If therapy gives you the feeling you're always right, you can say the most absurd or obscene things."

"Which is what you want a patient to do in a psychoanalytically oriented psychotherapy," I said. "To share all his thoughts, feelings, and fantasies, not just those that are conventional and well mannered. In sharing them, the patient becomes familiar with what he is really like, what inner demons he is struggling with, what warmth and sensitivity he has stifled."

Dr. B. returned to specific discussion of Renee's case. "Well, since you had the courage to speak up, tell us what you have been told about the boy you are about to see. Then we can discuss whether or not these 'facts' will help you to establish a genuine relationship with him."

"As I said, I know only a few facts," Renee responded. "He is seven, he sets fires, and his family used to live in this area. That's about all." Renee stopped but remembered another detail. "Oh, I know his first name. Simeon."

"Even knowing a patient's name can be problematic."

"Come on," Renee said. "You've made your point, Dr. B.! Now I think you are pushing it too far."

"That's not the case," Dr. B. replied. "Knowing a name can interfere with the relationship you hope to develop. I wasn't aware of this when I began at the Orthogenic School. But a number of children we treated eventually asked us to call them by a name other than the one they had been given. On reflection, I realized that all children who came to us should have this option. So as soon as a new child came to live with us, I asked what name they preferred we call them or if they wanted us to call them by a different name, one other than the one they had been given.

"Although quite a few liked the idea and changed their first names, the majority did not. Nearly all reacted positively to our offer. Overtly, many seemed to ignore it, but later, we learned that the offer had been very significant to them. They had understood that the school was offering them a new beginning, an opportunity for a different life, a different personality as it were, and this had been very encouraging and had made them believe that a new life was possible, even for them.

"Others, and their number was considerable, openly wondered why they had been given this option. That gave us a welcome opportunity to explain the purpose of psychotherapy: If they wanted, psychotherapy would help them change important aspects of their personality in ways they liked best, and for them, things did not have to remain as they were.

"If they felt their old name referred to their old personality and life, they might wish to have a new name to separate clearly the new life and new personality, which eventually would emerge with treatment, from the old one they would be shedding. Of course, names are only symbols. But they are important symbols. Our explanation helped children understand that psychotherapy would make accessible to them many ways in which to make themselves over, but only as they wished. It was a shorthand way of convincing them that from now on they could make big decisions about their lives.

When you already think of the child by his or her given name and accept this as solid knowledge, it is much more difficult to offer a child such an option spontaneously and to mean it.

"Let's say you do happen to know the child's name or learn it later on. Then it always is a good idea, if you can do so unobtrusively, to find out whom the child is named for, and whom the child reminds the parents of. These are latent identifications that parents have that strongly influence their reactions to the child."

For a moment Dr. B. appeared to be immersed in thought. "You also said that he sets fires. That's hearsay. How long will it be hearsay for you?"

"But his own mother told the evaluator that he did," Renee said.

"So his mother accused him of setting fires. What does the law say our attitude should be toward someone who is accused of a crime, such as arson?" Dr. B. said.

"Arson?" Renee said. "What do you mean, 'arson'?"

Bill was often provocative. "That's ridiculous," he said. "Renee said that the kid sets fires. You act like she called him a torch murderer."

"I repeat my question," Dr. B. said. "What does American law say we presume?"

"You're innocent until proven guilty," Jason replied.

"That's right," Dr. B. said. "When you consider it a fact that this boy sets fires, you condemn him for a crime on insufficient evidence and contrary to the presumption of innocence that our legal system grants to everyone. As the boy's therapist, shouldn't you be as biased in his favor as the law requires the court to be in regard to an accused?"

Renee looked dumbfounded. "You're just exaggerating. I never accused him of a crime!"

"Didn't you say that one fact was that he sets fires?" Dr. B. said.

Gina spoke softly, with a slight Italian accent. "Listen, Renee. It's similar to what we were discussing about parents, schools, and the records. Your little boy's mother is worried. Perhaps her son's been involved in a fire, little or big. She's scared, and she wants to be sure something is done. She doesn't want her house burned down.

"So right now, she perceives her son as a monster, and may give the boy's history based on her fears. You read what she said, and since a skilled evaluator put it in the record, it seems like a fact. If I were you, I'd be half-expecting this boy to burn down my office."

"I don't think that's what's on my mind, but . . ." Renee's voice trailed off.

"Let's say that you're not worried that he'll burn down your office," I said. "Even so, a report that he sets fires has to affect you. Setting fires is an important fact you should not overlook. So if you accept that he sets fires, how could you avoid using that 'fact' when you form some picture of what your patient is like? Perhaps he will feel only subliminally that you are suspicious of him. Then he will react to what he vaguely senses. After all, his mother has said he's done something very bad. If he feels guilty, he will try to be as devious as he can so that you will begin to doubt your suspicion. If he is more neurotic, he might act badly so you will punish him, since he feels guilty and feels he deserves to be punished if the orderly universe where crimes are punished is to be preserved. If he considers himself innocent, he will rightly be outraged and want to have nothing to do with you. Thus, when you meet him, having this prior information will make it difficult to know whether he is responding to you spontaneously or to the prejudices you greet him with."

Michael spoke up. "The students can't avoid information that gives them preconceptions. I think they need assistance to minimize the harm. Telling Renee how her preconceptions make it hard to listen open-mindedly just makes her even more anxious. I think she needs more direct help to get ready."

"Fair enough," Dr. B. replied. "Perhaps one of you has recently had a first meeting with a child. Let's listen to an account of this experience, and as we discuss it, perhaps we can draw some conclusions that will help Dr. Kurtz."

Jason rose to this challenge. He had grown up in Salt Lake City, a member of a prominent family that had been there almost since the late 19th century. He had already finished three years of adult psychiatry training at a famous midwestern hospital that had a strong psychoanalytic orientation. Child psychiatry is a subspecialty of general psychiatry, just as hematology is of internal medicine. He had come to Stanford for child psychiatric training because he wanted to work not only with adults and older adolescents but also with children.

"I had a first meeting a few days ago," Jason said. "The patient is eleven years old; her name is Margot, and she was brought to the hospital because she has lost a lot of weight recently. I met her in the social worker's office soon after Margot's parents agreed that Margot should be admitted and would stay in the hospital for a while. I introduced myself and explained that I would like to be alone with Margot while her parents arranged the admission."

"How did you say that to Margot?" Dr. B. asked.

"I said, 'The way I like to work is to meet with you for a few minutes so we can get to know each other while your parents are taking care of the admission procedures. Then we'll all get together to talk about what will happen next.' I explained that my office was a few doors down the hall and asked her to walk there with me. She followed me. I held my office door open for her and said, 'Please sit down anywhere.' She looked around and took a chair at the far end of the office."

"Could you describe your office?"

"It has several chairs against one side wall and a low table in the middle that has child-sized chairs all around it. Margot sat in the chair at the far end, so that the table was between her and the door. I sat down opposite her."

"Then what happened?"

"I said hello. She said hello shyly, kind of looked down, and didn't say anything else. I explained that the purpose of our short meeting was for me to get to know her and for her to get to know me a little better. I would be her doctor. I would talk to her three times a week and help her with any worries that she had. I also explained that from time to time I'd see her on the ward. I said that I knew almost nothing about her except that she had come to be treated. I asked why she had come now. She didn't respond at all. In fact, she looked kind of puzzled. So I said, 'What do you hope to be helped with?' "

Dr. B. looked at Jason skeptically. "Did she answer?"

"Contrary to what you seem to be thinking, yes, she did," Jason replied. "And quite impressively. She said, 'To get over my depression.' Her words surprised me. They sounded like what a sophisticated adult patient would say. I asked what her depression felt like. She said that for the past few months, she had felt sad and empty most of the time. She used to get excited about lots of things—jogging, ballet, horseback riding, playing the flute, writing stories, reading, making things in arts and crafts—but none of them was fun any more."

"What do you make of that?"

"That she is depressed."

"How does she look?"

"Depressed."

"Can you be more specific?"

"Well, she looks tired. 'Burnt out' might be the best description."

"Did she tell you any more about her behavior or feelings?"

"Only that she eats tiny portions of many foods, but feels very full after a few bites and worries about getting fat."

"Could you repeat what you said when you asked her to come to your office?"

"I said, 'I'd like to get to know you better, and to give you an opportunity to get to know me.'"

"Well, what opportunity to get to know you did you give her during the conversation you just told us about?"

Jason looked puzzled. "I already told you that. I told Margot a bit about how I work, that I'd spend a few minutes every day checking in with her, getting feedback on how things are going. At least three times a week we'd meet in the play room for forty-five minutes."

"That's it? That's all she's going to know about you?"

"That was all I was planning to tell her," Jason answered. "Of course, I want her to feel that I'm a kind and friendly person, but she has to discover that for herself. I already told her I'd help her with any worries, but she has to decide it's safe to talk to me. I hope she's begun to feel that."

"I hope so, too," Dr. B. said. "What do you think about this start you have made?"

"I'm pleased." Jason said. "I didn't expect an eleven-year-old to be so articulate about her feelings or so frank with me about her behavior. I felt reassured that my training with adult patients stood me in good stead. You know, from what she said, I really could sense how she feels when she is faced with a meal. She begins with an appetite, but each time she goes to take a bite, she's overwhelmed with a feeling of fullness and with worry about becoming fat. She seemed so bewildered and discouraged when she was telling me."

"Did you tell her you sympathized with her bewilderment?" Dr. B. asked.

"Not in so many words. But I listened attentively when she spoke, and I looked sympathetic, which she had to notice."

"You showed her that you were kind and friendly."

"Yes, I think I did."

"What else showed her this?"

"I hope, everything in my behavior. I tried to treat her respectfully. As I told you, I held the office door open for her; I invited her to sit wherever she liked, and I explained what we'd be doing together."

"I'm sure you treated her with great respect and listened to her with more attention and patience than most adults she's met till now," Dr. B. said. "She sounds like an astute youngster, and I'm sure she was aware of your kind intent. But most of the hospital's employees will be kind to her and quite a few will be friendly. How is she going to perceive you, her psychotherapist, as different from these others? Why will she want to bring her worries specifically to you?"

"Because he will be able to relieve them," interjected Renee. "That's how psychotherapy works."

"How has Dr. Winn shown this so far?" Dr. B. said.

"Jason said he's been friendly," Bill said.

"But how is Margot going to come to trust him, to know that he is her ally who wants to help relieve her anxieties? There is a big difference between being friendly and being a friend. That is what you may be having some trouble grasping. A friend, particularly in childhood, is someone who sees the world from your perspective." Dr. B. turned to Jason. "That is why you have to let Margot know very explicitly that *you* see the world from her perspective, or that at least you are trying to. Only when she knows that you are ready to see events and circumstances from her viewpoint, will she consider you a possible friend.

"In this regard, Margot's no different from the rest of us. We all listen to friends far more patiently and attentively than we do to anyone else. To have an impact as a therapist, you need to inspire this type of careful listening, so that what you say and do will have an impact on your patient, probably not right away, but over time."

Gina leaned forward. "But Jason showed his readiness to hear Margot's point of view. That's why she told him so much about her depression and the activities she once liked."

"I know how impressed you all are with Margot's articulate reply," Dr. B. said. "I am less so. Because I am not sure that what Margot told Jason was her own point of view. She seemed articulate and said things that probably were true. And like the rest of you, Dr. Winn was impressed because her words and self-knowledge seemed so mature. I'm not denying that Margot has lost her spark and wonders why she isn't interested in anything any more. And I agree that Dr. Winn is genuinely concerned and has a talent for conveying nonverbally that his caring is genuine. But when Margot spoke, it is quite possible that for the most part she was simply repeating what adults have said to her, which may be why she sounded so adult. Let us hope that Margot feels closer to her therapist for seeing on his face his willingness to share her pain. I want to suggest that other opportunities presented themselves in that interview for Dr. Winn to strengthen his alliance with Margot, but he doesn't seem to have been aware of them. So now, with your permission, I'd like to review what you've told us and discuss some ways in which you can build on this start."

"Sure," Jason said. "I'm here to learn."

"I'd like to return to the very moment your relationship with Margot began. If you do know the age of the child you are going to see, you should be able to reflect on how you felt at that age to make tentative hypotheses about her perspective. In that sense, before you ever met Margot, you had a way to identify with her more closely than I think you let yourself realize. After all, you've been eleven years old. You already have been through many of her experiences. Even if you were never brought to a hospital, as a child you surely were brought other places through no initiative of your own. Can you remember what you felt when your parents packed you into the car and brought you to some place you didn't want to go?"

"Resentment," Jason answered.

"Exactly. And that resentment overflowed to everyone associated with the occasion, even if they had had nothing to do with your being brought there. That's why it is likely that, in Margot's eyes, your association with this hospital makes you suspect. There she is in the social worker's office, angry at her parents for delivering her to this unfamiliar institution with its unfamiliar people, and along you come to invite her down the hall. Why would she want to go with you? However angry she is at her parents for consigning her like a parcel, wouldn't she still want to stay near them and try to figure out what they are up to?"

"But she did follow me willingly," Jason protested.

"Yes, she did. Doesn't that seem odd? If I were a stranger and approached you at a time when you were absorbed in something crucial to your future and told you that starting right at that moment, you and I would spend forty-five minutes three times a week to get acquainted, would you follow me willingly?"

"No, I suppose not," Jason said.

"And if I called your getting acquainted 'my work,' what would you think?

"I'd think you were crazy."

"Yes, you might. So why might you follow this stranger as Margot followed you?"

Jason sat looking at Dr. B. without saying a word.

"I think the only reason you would follow this stranger," Dr. B. continued, "would be because your situation was so miserable that anything would be an improvement, or because you were so dejected that you no longer cared what happened to you. Let's think about the phrase you used to explain yourself to Margot. 'The way I would like to work . . . ,' wasn't that it?"

Jason nodded.

"What does an eleven-year-old make of it that you call the relationship you want to form 'work'? From her perspective and understanding of language, doesn't that sound like you will do the work, as if she were a car and you were a mechanic? Do you hear how that allies you with those who treat her as a package? You expect her to be passive.

"Actually, you introduce another complication when you phrase your idea this way. When you say—I would like to work in some particular way without really inquiring what the girl might want—you immediately and unwittingly establish a dominant-inferior relationship. For the purpose of psychotherapy this is very undesirable. You put yourself in the dominant position, which is not lost on the patient who, we may assume from the little we know, already is resisting those whom she views as dominating her, and whom she thinks she cannot fight openly.

"One of the most fascinating hospitals I ever saw was a centuries-old Catholic hospital in a small French town. How do you think the patients were received in a good religious institution that a religious order ran? What was *their* first encounter with the hospital staff?"

When no one answered, Dr. B. went on. "One of the brothers took the patient, and they both went down on their knees and prayed together. Why did this old religious order take this approach? What does it tell the patient?"

"It accepts the patient as part of the fellowship," Jason replied.

"That's right. It openly declares their equality in front of God. Compare that with the inequality between doctor and patient that exists in our 'enlightened,' modern psychiatric hospitals, and in our assertions that we will be able to help the patient."

Jason seemed pained; Dr. B. tried to reassure him. "It takes courage to learn to do psychotherapy and to present cases in a seminar like this that focuses not just on the case but on you, the therapist. It is hard not to take these criticisms personally. But Dr. Rosenfeld and I can teach because we've made the same errors ourselves. Every experienced therapist has. I'm just using your case as an example to teach, knowing full well that 'most anybody would have done the same in this situation or worse."

"I'm glad you pointed that out." Jason settled back in his chair. "I know why I said what I did. I was feeling a lot of anxiety myself in the social worker's office."

"That's exactly what I'm talking about. Naturally you felt anxious. Almost all therapists feel some anxiety meeting a new patient. The problem is that you dealt with your anxiety at a moment when Margot should have been entitled to have her anxiety dealt with first. What happened then?"

"I explained that my office was right down the hall and asked her to walk there with me. I held the door open for her and said, 'Please sit down anywhere.'"

Dr. B. was silent for a moment. It struck me then that, nearing eighty, he was making familiar points to another generation of psychotherapists. How many times had he done this before? "Now what do you imagine an eleven-year-old girl thinks happens in a doctor's office?" Dr. B. valued answers that came from personal reflection, and he pointed Jason in that direction. "When you were an eleven-year-old boy and your parents took you to a doctor's office, what did you expect would happen there?"

"Something painful."

"Thank you. In this situation with Margot you knew what was going to happen in your office, but she did not."

Jason looked quizzical, so I expanded on this point. "Since Margot's parents had already agreed that Margot would be admitted to a hospital, she probably was acutely anxious about what medical procedures she would have to undergo. Some anorexics have been told that the hospital staff will use intrusive methods if the patient doesn't eat. But whether or not she knew that most hospitals use forced feedings or similar procedures with anorexics, she knew enough about hospitals, as do most children, to have vague fears about what might happen to her in one. Although you are familiar with the routine practice of telling a patient being admitted what procedures will be used, you didn't recognize that she might need assurances that you would not pass tubes down her nose to force-feed her.

"I think I know why you had this trouble. I still remember how hard it was to start my own child psychiatry training. After I had struggled for years to feel comfortable and a bit competent seeing adult patients, suddenly I was seeing children and was keenly aware that that feeling of inadequacy had returned. But it was more painful and poignant, since I had overcome the feeling in my work with adult patients and now was voluntarily subjecting myself to it again to enhance my skills so I could also treat children. If I were in your situation, I might have been so concerned with starting this psychiatric treatment the right way, a whole new endeavor with all the old insecurities, that I might have had a hard time involving myself with Margot's concerns and might have forgotten to give her the assurance I naturally would have given if I had felt more secure."

Jason nodded and said, "Bingo!"

I knew, from having interviewed Jason when he applied to the training program and from having spoken to his former teachers, that he was a kind man, concerned about patients' feelings, and deeply committed to quality care for children. But in this case, he had failed to project himself into Margot's situation and to act on the basis of his empathetic understanding.

"Doesn't your description of meeting with Margot remind

you of your own childhood experiences with doctors?" Dr. B. continued. "Margot followed you dutifully down the hall and into your office because that is how she relates to adults."

"But she did talk to Jason," Gina insisted.

"Yes, let's review that conversation. Do you remember that when Dr. Winn asked, 'What brings you here?' Margot looked puzzled. But when he said, 'What do you hope to be helped with?' she described her symptoms." Dr. B. paused and looked around. "What do you make of that?"

"I don't know what you're driving at," Jason said.

"It seems that she opened up," Gina said. Bill nodded in agreement.

"I don't see it that way," Dr. B. went on. "I have the impression that Margot did not answer your first question because she did not know how to. I also think that her second answer was not her own."

"But her second answer about her depression sounded so frank and to the point," Renee said. "I was impressed. She was so mature in describing her symptoms."

"Think carefully about what happened," Dr. B. said. "When Dr. Winn asked, 'What brings you here?' one part of Margot may have wanted to say, 'Go ask my parents; they're the ones who dumped me in the car and delivered me here; I'd rather be anywhere else.' Another part might have wanted to justify her parents' decision. She would have had to struggle with those competing tendencies. But then Dr. Winn asked, 'What do you hope to be helped with?' I would guess that these questions suggested to Margot which stance he expected her to take. So she complied and knew what to say. However, if I am reading her right, Margot doesn't think she needs help. Why should she want to be helped? Most anorexics want to be left to their own devices."

"I was presupposing that most anorexics also have a great deal of pain in their lives," Jason replied.

Dr. B. laughed wryly. "That they share with the rest of

humanity. The problem is what are the specific causes of this girl's great pain."

"I felt I was being helpful and fair. I said I would be her doctor who would talk to her and help her with any worries she had. I don't really see what's wrong with that," Jason said.

"Putting it in terms of being right or wrong isn't the relevant question," Dr. B. said. "What is relevant is whether what you said had a chance of furthering your psychotherapeutic relationship with Margot. Now when you tell Margot 'I'm going to help you with your problems,' doesn't it presuppose that she accepts that she has problems? I'm not so sure she really thinks she does, even if to be compliant she says that she does.

"Whenever I meet a new patient, I use a different tack. I say, 'What can I do for you?' and leave it up to her to tell me if there are problems for which she needs my help. Sometimes the answer is 'Nothing!' Then I accept that I was declared useless, because the assumption that I can help somebody with her problems is somewhat arrogant. I think that we do better approaching patients with some modesty. If, when I ask what can I do for her, the answer is 'Nothing,' I will say, 'That's too bad! Maybe if I try very hard I can do something, a little thing at least. I don't know if it's much.'

"If you approach children asking, 'How can I help you with your problems?' for many we treat, the only honest reply they could give is 'Give me a different father and mother.' What are you going to do with that?" Dr. B. asked rhetorically, and answered the question himself. "Your asking her to tell you about herself assumes that she easily can trust an adult and is willing to cooperate because she wants to be helped. This really is contrary to the little information you had, which is that she's only eleven years old, a young age for anorexia, and that her parents were with her. What I would ask this girl is not whether she wants or needs help, but I would stick with 'Why are you here?' She might answer something like, 'My parents forced me,' possibly adding, 'They're foolish!'

"We all resent being taken somewhere unless we know exactly why we are going or have specifically asked or at least agreed willingly to be taken. I would approach any child whose parents bring her to me on the basis of that resentment because that way I have a much better chance of establishing communication and getting acquainted.

"Sure Margot is suffering and is unhappy about having lost her appetite for life. What has happened in her feelings must bewilder her. But do you really think she was troubled enough to seek a psychiatrist's help of her own volition? Isn't it at least as likely that, now that she's here, she has decided to play the part of the dutiful child trying to adopt the rationale of adults who've thrust her into this situation?"

"I'm still not sure what you're telling me," Jason said.

Dr. B. explained: "I am saying that she is simply parroting her parents' words and attitudes. You might get an entirely different response with an alternative approach. You would be amazed by the information I have elicited, and the degree to which some children have gained confidence in me, when I simply asked: 'What's wrong with your parents that they brought you here?' Often it has opened up sluices of significant confidences."

Jason looked doubtful. "Wouldn't I be taking a big risk saying to Margot, 'What's wrong with your parents?' Other than my own memories of being brought to places at my parents' convenience, I had no indication that Margot was angry at her parents and certainly none that she was aware of her anger."

"That's true," Dr. B. said. "But from your description, I would feel confident guessing that she is at least baffled by them and resents being brought to the hospital. The approach I suggest does not work if you regard it as a technique or, worse, as a trick. What enables the child to open up with feelings about being misunderstood at home is her sense that her feelings are valid, and that you empathize with them."

Jason sat silently for a while. He looked at me. "I know that Dr. B. could say that to a kid and be comfortable. But I'm not as experienced and feel I need to be neutral."

"Sure you do," I said. "But since you had no idea to what degree Margot was allied with her parents, and since you knew it was possible that she was angry with them, isn't your question, 'What do you hope to be helped with?' as loaded as 'What's wrong with your parents?' Inadvertently, you showed her that your tendency was to side with adults."

"I think you're being too hard on Jason," Bill said. "He got Margot to reveal some of her pain, and he's shown his capacity to sympathize and accept."

"If I'm being too hard, it's because I know that Jason has a far greater capacity to empathize with Margot than he has shown her so far," I replied. "It's worth making the point because it is essential for all of you in your future work as therapists. Your life experiences are crucial, useful tools in carrying out psychotherapy. Only when you realize that your young patients are not so different from you, and recall how you saw the world at their ages and how you then would have seen what they are doing, does their behavior begin to make sense. If you can develop empathy with their life experiences and points of view, you begin to have a notion of how you appear to them and what messages your questions and responses convey about you and your attitude towards them.

"Let's go back to the admissions office. I doubt that most eleven-year-old children would be eager to leave the room in which their parents are making momentous decisions about their future. If Margot, like most anorexics, does not trust therapists, she might be even more keen to stay there and perhaps pick up a clue or two about what this hospital stay was going to be like. Sure she has fears about what the hospital staff might do to her; her parents' apprehension would reinforce these fears. Margot doesn't know when she will be going home, and she may not be sure how eagerly her parents will welcome her back. Even if they do not want to admit it to her or to themselves, her parents probably are angry at her. Not only has she been defying them at home by refusing to eat, but now she is shaming them in public. If they are psychologically unsophisticated, they may feel that going to the hospital exposes them as inadequate parents, unable to deal with a rebellious child. If they are sophisticated, they may expect the therapist to blame them for poor parenting and for causing Margot's illness. Either way, they are not in a position socially or emotionally to comfort Margot as they sign the admission papers.

"In the social worker's office, decisions are being made about her future. No one is explaining to her what is going on; she has to depend on her own eyes and ears to pick up clues. So at that moment, going a few doors down the hall to become acquainted with a stranger would not be tempting at all. Given all this, is there any message Jason could have given to Margot while she was in the social worker's office that would have gotten them to their private conversation just as quickly, but also would have shown Margot that he was offering her a special relationship?"

No one spoke.

Dr. B. prompted: "What was Margot feeling at that moment?"

Answers came from around the table.

"Anger."

"Nervousness."

"Curiosity."

"Apprehension."

"Alone and abandoned."

"She was probably feeling all of them," Dr. B. replied. "So

what could Dr. Winn have said that would release some of that tension by letting her know it's going to be all right; you're in good hands here?"

"Why would she believe anything he said?" Bill asked.

"Why indeed?" Dr. B. nodded at Bill. "Adults make an incredible number of statements to children to which they never live up. We all remember from our own childhoods how frequently adults talked for their own benefit and how rarely for ours."

"So what exactly are you saying?" Bill said.

"To ask yourselves what Margot needed to hear so that she could believe Dr. Winn's reassurance, if he had offered it, and so begin to control her anxiety. Put yourselves in her position. I think you answered that you would be expecting something painful. How would Margot have reacted if you had said, 'Being brought to the hospital must be pretty awful. Your parents are going to be busy signing papers for a few minutes, but if you come to my office, I'll tell you about what happens in a hospital'? By saying that, you already would have given Margot the opportunity both to begin to know you and to begin to see how you work. You would have shown her that you are a person who can see the world from her point of view, who knows what she is feeling, and who cares to make her feel better. And you would have given her a first glimpse that you are a person who deals in words and uses them to allay anxiety. This might have helped her believe that she's in good hands.

"If she had come to your office expecting an explanation of hospital procedures, the seat she chose might have taught you something. If she still had chosen to sit at the far end of the table, you might have hypothesized that she did this for protection from you or as a symptom of a desire to put distance between herself and others in all situations. But since, as it happened, she did not have any idea of what to expect in your office, we don't know if her choice of seat was expressing some general attitude or a fear that you might perform invasive procedures.

"What else can you remember from age eleven? What did you know about hospitals at that time in your life?"

"I guess I knew that people had operations there," Jason replied, "though I had only a vague idea that people were cut open and that parts of them were removed."

"Do you see how much you already know about Margot's world?" Dr. B. said. "You need to stay in that world at the same time as you assume the role of child psychotherapist. At the Orthogenic School, the staff spent a good part of at least *four days* explaining the school's procedures to each new child. We showed the child around and invited her to ask questions—about us, what we did, and why we did it— and to observe us and to form her own judgments about us. She would have done that anyway, but the fact that we thought it important and invited her to do so communicated that we wanted her to draw her own conclusions. By the end of the fourth day, we had learned a lot about the child both from her questions and from what she didn't question. We also learned from her reactions to what she saw and to our explanations.

"At our first meeting with a new child, we assured her that nobody at our institution would force her to do anything she did not like doing. We tried to be ingenious enough to put this in specific terms that related to what might be this particular child's main concerns. So if Margot had come to us, we would have promised that, while we would very much like her to eat and drink, nobody would force food into her. It was entirely up to her when and what she would drink or eat.

"Naturally, all anorexics had to test that promise and did so for twenty-four to forty-eight hours. When they had explored the situation and tested our intentions, they all began to eat and drink. At first and for some time, they did so only hesitantly—repeatedly testing whether we would insist on their eating and drinking. They also ate very idiosyncratically. But we persisted. In our experience, anorexics who overcame their illness then enjoyed as fine a life as anyone sitting around this table. So we were pleased to be able to treat them.

"One teenage girl came to us emaciated. All the food her parents had tried to make her eat was unacceptable for reasons she had not shared. The staff assigned to her sat with her for an entire night and day, trying to make her as comfortable as they could, without any effort to press food or drink on her. After she became convinced that we would not force her to eat or drink—and as a consequence of the positive relationship we had tried to establish with her—she finally let it slip that she just might try to eat a rare brand of canned tuna imported from Norway. We did not ask how much it cost or insist on knowing why she could not accept a substitute. She was a starving girl, and we were delighted that there was some food we could get for her.

"For weeks she ate only this expensive tuna. She began to gain weight and to build up her strength because she ate both the fish and the oil in which it came. Only months later, when we had more fully won her confidence, did she share the secret of why she could eat that particular tuna: It came from Norway, a peaceful country that, in her opinion, had never participated in any imperialistic ventures and had not exploited any people of the third world. Because she considered her wealthy parents' politics exploitative of developing countries, the food they offered her was unacceptable, and since she feared others were in cahoots with her parents, she would not tell anyone else why she refused food.

"After she shared her reasons, we easily found food imported from either the third world or the very few other nations she considered 'good' countries. That made it simple to enlarge her diet. Eventually, the lengths to which we went to cater to her idiosyncratic food choices impressed her, but it took about a year of this food and repeated tests of our intentions before she ate an unrestricted diet. Even then, for a year or two we continued to supplement her diet with food from 'good' countries to show her that we respected her ideals and had not just been humoring her.

"Now, in these early months and years, we never tried to interpret her concern for the weak of the third world as perhaps also reflecting her feelings about how her powerful parents had treated her as a weak child. Had we interpreted this meaningful displacement early on, she might have considered us intrusive and condescending, when in fact the staff really had great respect for her idealism.

"Margot also is entitled to receive information about our treatment methods and intentions right away. She needs to know that her psychiatrist will get his information not from physically intrusive methods, but from what she tells him of her own volition. Unless she's had previous experience with psychotherapy, she is likely to expect that you are just another doctor who will manipulate her and tell her what she must and must not do."

"If we try to do special things in our hospital like you did with that girl," Gina said, "we get arguments about how these special foods or toys are too expensive."

"So did we, though the questions became fewer over the years. We always presented our arguments in relation to the cost of one day in the school. A month of this tuna cost less than one day at the school. Although it seems self-evident, many administrators overlook this. An insurance company will budget one thousand dollars to pay for a child to stay in the hospital for one day, but they will balk when minor sums are spent on special foods or for toys as presents. Yet these small items are wonderful investments. If they shorten the patient's stay by one hour, they will have paid for themselves."

Dr. B. paused a moment and said to Jason, "When I seem

so critical of how you proceeded with Margot, please do not take it personally. I would not waste the group's time discussing the chance errors of an individual. We all make our own mistakes all the time, myself included. But the issue we are discussing today is both general and critical: Why do we behave with very disturbed children in a manner which we know is wrong when we are subjected to it ourselves?"

Jason sighed and looked visibly relieved. "Because psychoanalytically oriented psychotherapy is hard to explain."

"Exactly," said Dr. B. "It's hard enough to explain the hows and whys of child psychotherapy to ourselves or to interested adults. So how can we expect to be able to easily explain it to a very disturbed, confused, anxious child who is apt to misinterpret what we are saying in line with her own natural anxieties, if not also her delusions? Our only hope is to make a very good job of explaining ourselves, our methods, and our intentions to her.

"Obviously we cannot explain all—or even the more important ins and outs of psychoanalytically oriented treatment—to a new patient, least of all to an anxious child, like Margot, on first meeting her. It won't do to tell her that one of our goals is to relieve her anxiety, although it is. Because it is a rare child who would believe us. Nor does the statement that our purpose is to get to know each other make much sense to the child, because she has had experiences that prove that while adults feel quite free to ask her all sorts of questions about herself, they usually are not all that ready to answer when she questions them.

"Now what do we know from everyday life? Often, when we open up about ourselves, our companion will, in response, open up about herself. So instead of suggesting that getting to know each other begins with the child talking about herself, or my asking her questions about herself, it is better to start by telling the child something about me and how I do things.

"Some child therapists want to start treatment by saying,

'I want to be your friend.' That doesn't make sense to me. If I were a seven-year-old and you said, 'I want to be your friend,' I'd say, 'I would prefer a kitten.' Children say 'I want to be your friend' only in primers. If you watch how children make friends, you'll see a child approach another, point at a neutral object or activity, and say, 'Look at that.' So you're better off when the child asks you why you are seeing her, to say, 'I want to learn, and you're a good one to teach me.' That puts the child in control of the situation and is honest.

"While my intention on first meeting a child is to make myself known to her, unless she asks me specific questions—which happens occasionally but is rare—I tell her something about my procedures. In doing so, I hope to be ingenious enough to address myself to some major anxiety the child is likely to suffer from and that this situation has activated. My desire is to reassure her. But I won't come out and tell her that directly. It would be too clumsy and likely would not be believed. Instead, I simply tell her about some of the things I plan to do. From this, much more than from anything I could say about me personally, the child forms her opinions about what I am up to, maybe even what I might be like.

"It is somewhat different with psychotic individuals, particularly younger children, who do not respond favorably to what you tell them. They have very good reasons to distrust what they are told. Psychotic individuals have all had such bad experiences with what people tell them, they have learned to trust what they see or, in an even deeper way, what they smell. So how you prepare the environment you will see them in and how you greet them is most important.

"After I have explained a few things to the child, I tell her that I do not know what else she might be interested in, but that I would be happy to tell her what she wants to know. In this I invite her questions. That usually works. If not, I continue to explain myself.

"I also invite the child to look around the place, that is to investigate the premises. And to most children I certainly offer cookies and candy right away. This usually tells the child more about me in an important area than anything I can say in words.

"At the Orthogenic School, when a new child came to see me, I assumed she might have been brought to me against her will. So I nearly always started explaining myself to her long before I dared to suggest to the child that she explain herself to me. I made it clear that at all times she was free to leave whenever she wanted to and that we would make no effort to restrain her from doing so. Many children tested this promise and walked out. But with the exception of one child, they all came back as soon as they had convinced themselves that I wouldn't make any move to bring them back. But I do admit that as they left, I tried to push some candies into their hands."

"Aren't you asking too much of me or any other trainee here?" Jason said. "You had a staff and control. I don't have the Orthogenic School's resources at my disposal."

"But you do have your sensitivity and intuition, Jason," I said. "You showed us that you can be in touch with your eleven-year-old self. You had a deep empathy with Margot's feeling about eating and gave me a clear idea of what you thought Margot was experiencing. But this morning, your own anxiety interfered with letting Margot see that side of you even though it would have contributed to establishing a empathic rapport with her.

"These are issues we all confront every time we meet a new patient. If you assume that, however anxious you feel, the new patient is more anxious, and I think that is a safe assumption, you may feel more at ease, more able to pay attention to their anxieties. If you had made that assumption, Jason, you probably would have felt freer to focus on Margot and your shrewd observation that she looked burnt out. Not all anorexics look burnt out. Some do, while others, like the one I saw when I was a beginning psychiatric resident, seemed to be bubbling over with energy."

"From the list of the activities Margot used to participate in, I would assume that she was doing far too much," Dr. B. interjected. "At a recent get-together of Nobel Prize winners, the animal ethologist Niko Tinbergen spoke of the vast increase in infantile autism in the United States and other Western countries. He believes that the cause of this autism is the absence of positive communication between mother and infant. He felt that another factor in the increase is the result of Western parents, educators, and psychologists expecting children to do too much."

"Which shows what happens when Nobel prize winners go butting into someone else's field," Bill said.

Everyone laughed. Then Dr. B. went on: "Well, Dr. Winn still came very close to recognizing the phenomenon that Tinbergen commented on." Dr. B. spoke directly to Jason. "Perhaps if you had felt freer to trust your perceptions, you would have said something to Margot like, 'Poor girl! You were doing too much. You're completely exhausted. It's high time for you to take a good, long rest.'

"This phenomenon you noticed has wide application and is one prevailing source of childhood psychopathology in America's middle class. Often, parents whose children are overloaded with activities display a disquieting indifference to their child as an individual combined with an insistence on very high performance. For such children, psychotherapy aims to free them of their preoccupation with performance, to emphasize not achievement but who they are as people. Through her experience with her therapist, Margot ought to be able to discover that she has open to her the possibility of an undemanding relationship with a person who accepts and respects her for who she is.

"When you give back to the patient what she has communicated to you, for instance telling her that she has been doing too much and needs a rest, she recognizes that you have focused on and really listened to her. Then she may glimpse the notion that psychotherapy actually might offer a unique relationship. The process of therapy begins when the child begins to wonder about the nature of what she is starting."

"What do you mean by 'the child begins to wonder'?" Renee asked. "How do we know when the process of therapy begins?"

"It begins when the child recognizes that the therapist is listening to her more carefully than she listens to herself, and wonders why," Dr. B. said. "She begins to listen too, both to herself and to the therapist. And this awakened curiosity —this listening to and taking herself more seriously—is when therapy begins. For curiosity to be aroused, the child has to experience the therapist's unique awareness. What we have been exploring are the moments in Dr. Winn's interview with her when this intensity was allowed to dissipate.

"So, has this discussion influenced your view of your relationship with Margot?"

Jason smiled at Dr. B. "It hasn't been my most comfortable experience." He was silent for a moment. "I'm not exactly pleased with what you made me notice. Should I thank you for helping me hear how stuffy I sounded?" Jason laughed. "Yes, I guess I should. I really wasn't being myself, or the therapist I am with adults. And I was unfair to Margot in not telling her what will and will not be done to her. I'm surprised at myself! Providing that information is standard admissions procedure with an adult patient. I guess I wasn't showing her as much respect as I thought.

"But you encouraged me to plan for tomorrow. I like the four-day orientation you gave new children at the Orthogenic School. What do you think of a condensed version? Tomorrow, I could take Margot on a stroll around the ward and encourage her to ask questions about what she sees. I could answer them as well as I can and explain to her which procedures are relevant to her case and which are not. Then, if there's time, we could go to the playroom, and she could observe the contrast between our work together and what happens on the ward."

"That sounds like an excellent idea," I said. "You'd be allaying her anxiety and introducing her to the therapeutic process at the same time. First, through what you do, you'll be showing her that as her therapist, you are a person who tries to understand her needs and has spent time thinking about how to meet them. You have described her as probably dejected. Without ever saying a word, the fact that you consider her important enough to think about when you're not with her would bolster her self-esteem.

"But that approach will give Margot other messages too. You'll show her that in psychotherapy we learn to allay anxiety by establishing the facts. You'll be encouraging her to observe, use her intellect, and ask questions until she understands what she sees, feels, and fantasizes. Thus, she'll be able to feel less anxious about being here. By unspoken analogy, she will glimpse how the two of you are going to explore her life and try to bring her other anxieties into the scope of the comprehensible world. Gradually, through using her very good mind, she will develop better ways of mastering anxiety than through anorexic symptoms."

Jason looked pleased.

"And since you are remaking your beginning with Margot," I added, "why not start with an apology for not responding to her anxiety yesterday? You've told us you feel sorry. Why not tell her? She might realize that you are a sensitive, thoughtful, genuine person worth forming an alliance with!"

Jason smiled.

I thought we ought to get back to Renee's case. "Has Jason's presentation helped you think more clearly about the boy you'll be seeing tomorrow?" I asked her.

"Yes and no," Renee replied. "The discussion convinced me that even a first session could give me a unique opportunity to begin building a relationship. But I can't say I feel reassured, certainly not comfortable or confident."

"What I'm about to say may sound paradoxical," I said, "but the way you feel tells me that you *are* closer to being ready for tomorrow. Let me expand on an analogy Dr. B. uses. You ought to prepare for a new patient the way you prepare for an honored guest in your home. Let's say you are expecting, not friends, but friends of friends to drop by your home around lunchtime. You may feel anxious because you want to receive them as graciously as possible, but you don't know anything about what foods they like or whether they will have eaten or not. You decide to prepare foods they might like. Because you don't want them to feel uncomfortable about your preparations or obliged to eat just to please you, you leave the prepared food in the refrigerator.

"When the guests arrive, since you have readied yourself as well as you can, you can focus on them. If they protest that they are not hungry, you will do your best to interpret their words. Do they mean what they say, or are they trying to be polite, to adapt themselves to what they believe to be your comfort? You have no vested interest in either eventuality, so only goodwill motivates you. You still may make mistakes. But your readiness frees you to be alert to please, thus creating an atmosphere in which this potential friendship between you has the best chance of getting off to a good start.

"Renee, I would imagine that some of the information you were given about the boy made you anxious before you ever met him."

"Like the fire-setting," Renee said.

"A perfect place to start," I said. "Fire-setting is a red flag to every therapist, a symptom you have to attend to. If serious fire-setting has taken place, as likely as not the police will be involved. But you don't know that yet. And for now, this information will interfere with getting to know the boy in an unprejudiced way.

"Is the allegation that he set fires really specific knowledge? Can't you picture a dozen ways in which a fire could have happened? Maybe what his mother calls starting a fire was being found lighting a match or a candle. We've seen cases like that. In those cases his being called a fire-setter is interesting only because it reveals that his mother is afraid of him. Could an older boy have set a fire and then run away, leaving this boy to take the blame? Could he have been playing Desert Island in a dangerous place? Maybe he never had any intention of starting a fire and now feels guilty and morbidly depressed because of all the trouble he has caused and is in. Then again, might he have been scared of the dark and, being immature, not realized what he was doing? Or in a sensual vein, might he have been playing with matches for the beauty and excitement, and then have run away when he thought someone was coming, not realizing he had actually started a fire? If there was a fire at all, was it belligerent, defensive, or accidental? Was the boy angry, hurt, and wanting to pay back some other person, or was he scared of someone and trying to protect himself? Was he trying to give someone an important message?

"When you have pictured all these possibilities as concretely as you can, you will know that you are ready for them all. You will realize that if the boy did set fires, his behavior has both a context and a meaning that you want to understand. Without them, you can't know if he set fires, and if he did, what they say about him as an individual.

"For instance, a colleague of mine told me about a boy who lived at a residential treatment center. The boy's parents were divorced, and the staff had the distinct impression that the mother was harsh and rejecting. She never had a good word to say about her son. His father was a passive man who at least had something approaching a good relationship with the boy. So the staff was pleased when the father wanted to improve that relationship and asked to take the boy on a weekend trip. The boy came back to the residential center on Monday. Tuesday morning he carefully and secretly set a very serious fire that almost burned down the cottage he had been living in. When the psychiatrist interviewed the boy, he refused to say why he had set the fire. Furthermore, he showed no remorse and would not even say that he would not set another fire.

"Since letting the boy continue to live in an open setting seemed unsafe, the staff sent him to a locked psychiatric unit in a hospital. He ended up going to several hospitals after that and had experiences that he later reported had been terrible and untherapeutic. Not until fifteen years later, after his life had been terribly adversely affected, did he reveal that on the Sunday before he set the fire, on that supposedly therapeutic trip, his father had sodomized him, a fact he could not tell anyone.

"So until you get to know the boy you'll see tomorrow, since so many scenarios are possible, keep your mind open so you will be able to pay attention to the real child who will come to see you. After you have seen the boy once or twice, after you have formed your own opinion of him and his behavior, study his record to see what those who have evaluated him originally thought about him and his problems. If their evaluation conforms to yours, you'll feel reassured. But if the evaluation differs from what you then will know about the boy, it will permit you to contrast the impression the boy made on that evaluator, with how he looks to you and you can try to figure out why these two impressions are different."

"I don't understand," Gina said. "Are you saying that all this imaginative preparation is supposed to help Renee dismiss the fires from her mind altogether at the first meeting?"

"No," I replied. "I'm saying that his mother might call so many situations 'fire-setting' that Renee ought to just interact, observe, and bring out the appropriate hypothesis when and if it seems relevant. If that approach does not suit Renee's style, she might share with her new patient what she's been told about him. Many therapists start this way to let the child know from the beginning that they will not have secrets from him. If you adopt that approach, it's worth adding that you are sure that what you have been told is far from the whole story. Encourage the child to tell you his side because you really want to hear it from him."

"Let's say this boy actually did set a bad fire," Dr. B. said. "Probably nobody's asked Renee's boy why he set the fire. You have to start there. Saying 'Don't set fires; it's wrong to set fires' only tells the child that you are not interested in him, that the only interest you and the world have is that he shouldn't cause trouble. With fire-setters you hardly ever hear the questions asked, 'Why did he set the fire? Why did he set it at that time? Why did he set it in that place? What was he trying to achieve?' I'm sure he had what he considered a valid reason. Nobody grants these children that they're reasonable human beings with what to them seem like sound motives for setting a fire. But if rather than just helping him to stay out of trouble, we are trying to heal him, we first have to know the answers to all those and many more questions.

"Whatever you decide to say in that first meeting, Dr. Kurtz, do remember the analogy between your preparation and that of a good host.

"An experience in my early days at the Orthogenic School made me keenly aware of how important it is that food, particularly cookies and candies, be freely available to children in treatment. My predecessor had a cabinet behind his desk in which he kept goodies locked up. One morning, I found a meat cleaver on my desk. During the previous night, some children at the school had used this cleaver to break open the candy cabinet. They had helped themselves to goodies and left behind a note to me that said, 'This time it's on your desk. Next time it will be in your head.'

"While I wasn't really scared that they would carry out this threat, I understood what they were communicating. I made it clear to all the Orthogenic School's students that from this moment on, the candy and cookies would be placed in an unlocked closet. They would be free to help themselves to what they wanted at any time, day or night.

"Over the years, this candy closet became an important institution, both in making the children feel welcome and in giving them the message that not only would their need for food always be met but also their desires for pleasant food would also be satisfied at their leisure. After this, I instituted a daily meeting with all patients at the Orthogenic School in which they were encouraged to suggest improvements and changes they wished to make in the program, including facets they felt ought to be discontinued because they didn't like them. These meetings became an important vehicle for increasing mutual understanding between the patients and the staff. I found them extremely useful in improving their program. And they had an added benefit: They gave our patients the sense that they were in charge of effecting changes for the better in their lives."

"I think that was what Jason intended when he let Margot choose a seat first," Gina said. "He wanted to make her feel comfortable."

"Yes," I said. "Jason undoubtedly learned in his adult training that it's important to let any new patient sit near the door in case they feel the need to escape. But with Margot, you forgot about the seating," I said to Jason. "Luckily she wasn't paranoid and aggressive. Paranoid patients may feel suspicious, trapped, and can get panicked. If you get between them and the door, they can get violent. Words of welcome won't make that much of an impression on them. So you do not want to block their escape route."

Dr. B. carried this idea forward. "Let me expand on something I said earlier. With psychotic children, you have to also pay attention to something else. They will pay close attention to how the room is decorated and how it smells. If you go to a new place, you also trust your sensual reactions, even though they may not be as insistent all the time to you as a psychotic's are to him. So, plan a room to be a good reflection of you. Make the chairs comfortable, and the candy and toys inviting and accessible. Do not keep things around that the child cannot play with freely, or which you will have to police. Your goal is to make the experience comfortable for the child, just as with guests coming to your home."

"Another thing," I added. "I know trainees here have to share offices, so you don't have absolute control over what's in the office and what shape it's in. But remember that children speak through toys and play. In our work with adults we follow the train of their thoughts. With children, we follow the flow of play and what interrupts it. But we can do that freely only if the toys we present do not intrude on the child's freedom of feeling and thought. Even a dollhouse can convey attitudes of considerate hospitality or thoughtlessness. If you plan to use a dollhouse in that first session, make sure you set it up before you bring the child into the room. Be certain that the dolls and furniture you use with the house are in good condition. Set the dollhouse and people up in some way that you think will be relevant to the child.

"If the room is not set up to greet the child, the child doesn't know what to make of what is presented to him. What does a kid think if he comes to a first session and sees that the therapist has left two entire families in the house? 'Does he think I have two mothers and fathers?' If his parents have divorced and both have remarried, the two families may be particularly relevant, but the child who lives with both parents will be bewildered. If you look in some of the offices, perhaps ones that you use, you'll see some of those flexible stick figure dolls with an arm torn off and just the bare inner wire sticking out. What is a child to make of the therapist's confronting him with a maimed individual? That figure will raise fears of amputation or castration, for example, that may have no relation to the child's central anxiety. How can you recognize what in the child's internal life or home environment is troubling him if you yourself create troubling questions? In contrast, when the dolls are intact and appropriate, they convey the message that children are welcome and that the therapist made an effort to obtain the kind of toys that children like to play with.

"Gradually, as you begin to know a child patient better during further sessions, you can prepare for him more specifically. As time after time you lay out the appropriate combination of adult, child, and baby dolls in representative situations, your message changes from, 'I understand and care about children like you,' to 'I think about you when you're not here; I remember what is important to you because it is important to me.' When children see that they have been prepared for, they can pick up where they left off in the last session or change the topic and play a new game."

Dr. B. looked at Renee. "All these suggestions are within the powers of a beginner. Your personality, experiences, and compassion are your most important tools. Use them to enter your patient's world. And remember that forging a friendship is a slow process. Don't be too hard on yourself when you emerge from that first meeting with only a few insights about your patient. If you have conveyed that you want him to be comfortable and that you are trying to see what he sees and to feel what he feels, over time he will give you many opportunities to learn through your listening and watching.

"Let me give you one last suggestion: Spend some time before tomorrow trying to see the world through the eyes of a seven-year-old. If you have a sense of how large the world appears to him and how powerful you seem in his eyes, you will have far less trouble attending to his anxiety before yours. You need to get the child's perspective. When I was starting out at the Orthogenic School, I spent time walking on my knees. I figured that crouching down to a child's height and observing what the world looks like to him would be invaluable preparation for entering a child's world and seeing it from his point of view. Wouldn't that be a good way to prepare for your first meeting tomorrow? If you do that and think about what you observe, you may realize, as I did, that the ceiling heights in our homes and offices are built for adults. That's why, on their own, children build little tents and playhouses with very low ceilings, according to their own dimensions.

"This problem holds for the child therapy rooms we use. Essentially, they are rooms built for adults that we try to fit, in some fashion, for children. If these rooms really were designed for children, they would be very different. Most children prefer to sit on the floor, under the table or desk, and so on. This is because they feel more comfortable in there, more protected in these confined places.

"So see how you would feel sitting under a desk if you were three and a half feet tall. What does your office look like from that perspective? Maybe you can make some simple adjustments—in addition to the child-sized chairs you have, bring the toys down low so that your patient will feel more comfortable, and he will see you have prepared for him."

At this, Renee smiled: "Well, now I do feel more ready to start. See you next week."

CHAPTER TWO

Punching Bags and Lifesavers

I CAME TO STANFORD with an established expertise in the problems abused children have. Therefore, I was particularly interested when a session discussed such a child. One week, Saul Wasserman, Director of the Child and Adolescent Psychiatric Inpatient unit at San Jose Hospital (known as CAPI for short), presented an abused child to the seminar. I had met Saul because I went to CAPI once a week to supervise my child psychiatry fellows who were spending six months of their two-year training program on the unit.

Ever since Saul had been a psychiatric resident at Stanford, he had been interested in society's outsiders: rough, tough kids, bona fide juvenile delinquents. In the 1970s and early 1980s, San Jose Hospital was a typical, financially strapped city hospital; the staff struggled for every square foot to accommodate a heavy patient load, much of it indigent. CAPI cared for twenty-six disturbed and disturbing children at a time. When Saul took over the unit in the mid-1970s, CAPI's treatment model was mainly behavioral, the shaping of a child's behavior so that it conformed to the minimal expectations of civilized life. Saul knew that behavior modification was relatively simple to implement, and it was particularly useful to him as a new unit director because it allowed him to achieve an organized, orderly, safe program with his relatively untrained staff.

However, Saul knew it was not the ultimate answer because it did not achieve the kinds of real internal changes in children that would endure. Because my own approach to these children was psychodynamic, I frequently found myself challenging CAPI's behavioral approach in frank, friendly discussions with Saul.

In 1981, I conducted a study with Graehem Emslie, a child psychiatry fellow at Stanford. We documented that over forty percent of CAPI's child and adolescent patients had been overtly mistreated physically or sexually prior to admission. The abuse had not been subtle. These children had been beaten till their bones broke, raped by their caretakers, thrown down the stairs by their mothers (for such innocuous childhood behavior as taking an apple out of the refrigerator), or locked in a closet for days.

These findings documented what Saul had begun to suspect. He reviewed the charts of all children who had been put in seclusion on the unit and realized to his horror that a large portion had been previously abused in their homes. The behavioral solution of putting a child patient in a "seclusion" room to "cool off" seemed dangerously close to locking him in a closet. Clearly, an approach that so closely reenacted their original trauma was not likely to heal their wounds. Saul began to pay increasing attention to the feelings prior maltreatment had aroused in CAPI's children, trying to understand the reasons behind the children's actions rather than simply trying to get them to behave better. We began to agree more on the way to approach abused children. In the late 1970s, I told Saul that my weekly meetings with Dr. B. and the seminars were changing the way I thought about troubled, abused kids. I invited him to attend.

First, with some trepidation, Saul invited Dr. B. to visit CAPI. After Dr. B. toured the unit, Saul mentioned that he wanted to install a punching bag because CAPI's kids were so angry at the world that they needed a way to work out their anger other than hitting the staff. Dr. B.'s response was typical of his style: "Well, if you think that way, there's some hope for you."

It took Saul several years of acquaintance with Dr. B. to understand fully what he had meant by this backhanded compliment. Dr. B. was pleased that Saul was offering the children a chance to discharge their anger safely, which meant that he thought their rage was understandable in light of their past experiences. But he also was observing that Saul expected an inanimate punching bag to do something for the child that can be achieved only through interacting with a caring human being. He knew that Saul's expectation that deprived and maltreated children could come to terms with their rage when they first entered CAPI simply by hitting a punching bag was a denial of the hard work we call the therapeutic process, in which learning to tame one's anger, to channel it constructively, is one prime goal.

Saul himself came to realize that in other ways a punching bag could short-circuit the therapeutic process. Letting a child take out his anger on the punching bag would spare Saul and his staff the hard work and self-scrutiny they needed to do to find out what *they* might have done to provoke the child, insignificant as that might be compared to what the child had suffered in the past. After all, these children did not hit all of the time. By ascribing the outburst of rage entirely to the child's past experiences, Saul might avoid exploring the present circumstances of the outburst and miss an opportunity to increase the level of understanding between the child and the CAPI staff.

When Saul came to our seminar to discuss a problematic CAPI case, he had a good opportunity to see how Dr. B.'s very different approach could work for him at CAPI.

"I'm confronting a situation I especially wanted to talk over with you," Saul said. "Bobby is a twelve-year-old boy who kicked in a door and set a fire in the kitchen of a crisis center he had been sent to for a cooling-off period."

"Well, isn't that what a crisis center is for, Dr. Wasserman?" Dr. B. asked.

"They like *quiet* crises," Saul replied. "Initially, Bobby was expelled from school for fighting with teachers. He frequently spent time smashing up furniture at home, and made himself popular with the fire department by setting fires in the neighborhood. His mother told us that Bobby had been a problem since he was three years old. However, since she also told us that Bobby had been an unwanted child, and that she and Bobby's father divorced before Bobby's first birthday, we suspect that Bobby has been a problem for them since before he was born."

"Where has Bobby been living?" I asked.

"His parents immigrated here from Belgium and separated a few months later," Saul answered. "Bobby spent his first ten years with his mother. But because his behavior was so difficult, she sent him to his father. While there, Bobby repeatedly showed up at school covered with welts and bruises. Eventually his father admitted that he beat Bobby regularly, to try to control him. Therefore, when Bobby turned twelve, child protective services returned him to his mother, who, needless to say, wasn't exactly overjoyed to have him back. Things went from bad to worse, and she turned Bobby over to child protective services. Within a few days of his getting to a crisis center, he started a fire in the kitchen. The fire department put it out. The police investigated, and, as I said before, he was transferred to CAPI. We were supposed to do what we always do in these cases. We are the triage station, evaluating children like Bobby, beginning their treatment, and working to get them into the best possible rivulet in the state's inadequate system for troubled children.

"When our staff reviewed Bobby's records, they found that at some time or another in this boy's life, he had received every treatment, proven or experimental—amphetamines, Dexedrine, Ritalin, even the Feingold diet—all of which had failed to improve his behavior."

"You mean the Feingold diet didn't cure him?" Dr. B. feigned horror. "I'm shocked!"

When our laughter subsided, Saul continued. "My unit is divided into two teams, each responsible for half the cases. I am head of Team B. Bobby spent his first thirty days in the hospital being cared for by Team A. They tried to provide a predictable, nurturing environment and attempted to control some of the negative things Bobby did by placing mild sanctions on them. But the staff couldn't get a picture of what was going on in Bobby's head and was getting more and more frustrated. They had problems with the way he acted. For example, he continually refused to attend classes."

"A most understandable sentiment," Dr. B. said. "I also often hated school but did not have the guts to be truant. If I had had the guts and school avoidance had been a reason for hospitalization, I would have spent twelve years in a hospital. But tell me, Dr. Wasserman. What does the boy look like? I can't picture him."

"He's small and observant with reddish hair, freckles, and blue eyes. He's shorter and more slender than most of the twelve-year-olds we've had on the unit, but the staff has found him a pain in the butt. They just can't set limits on him. Bobby did all right until he thought he didn't deserve some restriction. Then, quick as a light switch, he turned so hostile and antagonistic that the usually unflappable staff became angry and punitive. They were getting worn down; Bobby also was distressed. He already sees himself as a bad child, and these confrontations make him feel even worse."

Dr. B.'s measured voice seemed to indicate he had something in mind. "How did the staff *feel* about this boy?" When Saul and I discussed Dr. B.'s comment years later, we realized that Dr. B. already knew exactly who Bobby was and what he needed from a therapeutic setting. But his task as a Socratic teacher was to work out why Saul was not seeing it.

"Most like him, or at least wanted to," Saul responded, "but they were frustrated. Bobby disrupted the entire unit. Even when staff made special efforts to work with him, they got nowhere. Team A was ready to transfer Bobby's care, so when I offered to take him, they were more than willing. Right around that time, I was also taking care of a teenaged girl who, the staff kept telling me, was very much like Bobby. She also had been beaten by her parents and locked in a closet for days at a time. After the social service department took her away from her parents, they placed her in several foster homes and then in two residential treatment centers, none of which could cope with her. By the time she came to us, she'd been through the mill.

"I experimented doing some unorthodox things with the girl. For instance, she had trouble getting up in the morning. So I gave her a pack of Lifesavers and told her that as soon as she got out of bed, there would be a pack of Lifesavers for her. And I told her that if she wasn't getting other things she needed, she could give herself a Lifesaver. After several weeks, when she became convinced she could get a steady supply of Lifesavers from me, she started succeeding in the program and didn't need the Lifesavers.

"I decided to modify this approach and to try it with Bobby. The first morning he was assigned to my team I told Bobby, 'I know you feel you have nothing to look forward to. So tomorrow morning and every morning after that I'm going to give you a pack of Lifesavers.' He liked that. When he blurted out that he wanted a present, I told him that at two o'clock I'd be back with one.

"At two o'clock on the button, Bobby strutted up and asked me where his present was. He was sure I'd forgotten. But I had bought him one of those dollar ninety-eight windup panda bears that clang cymbals. Well, happiness is one thing—Bobby was ecstatic. I thought that was a pretty good sign. So I told Bobby he would get another present over the weekend and made sure that he did. I didn't give him anything Monday, but this morning I gave him a little set of toy soldiers. He asked if the pack had a tank in it. Luckily it did, which made the gift just perfect."

Dr. B. sipped his coffee and asked, "So what's the problem?"

"Six days of being easier to live with doesn't solve his problem. The minute he's frustrated, he still blows up."

Dr. B. spoke softly. "You want miracles?"

"No," Saul said and hesitated for a moment. "You don't believe me, do you? Well I'd be glad if we could do enough so Bobby doesn't end up in a locked facility."

"Do you really think a week is sufficient time to undo twelve years of deprivation?" Dr. B. said steadily. "In a week you can expect only so much. It's reasonable to estimate that it will take as long to undo the damage as it took to create it. If it takes less, everyone will be pleased, but to me that time estimate seems reasonable."

Saul looked at Dr. B. and around at the group and spoke urgently. "CAPI's not like the Orthogenic School. We don't have the luxury of that kind of time. In a month or two, Bobby will go to something like a long-term group home for boys. I don't want him to go feeling hopeless about his situation. I'd feel better if I could just give some helpful ideas to the person who will be working with Bobby next."

Dr. B. replied, "Okay. If you answer a question I asked

you, Dr. Wasserman, you might get some ideas to pass on. *How does your staff feel about this boy?"* When Saul remained silent, Dr. B. explained. "This youngster has been extremely deprived from the moment he was born. Your staff saw you give the girl Lifesavers and presents. If they liked this boy well enough and thought these two children were similar, why didn't they get the idea to give him presents?"

"It was an experimental idea, so I can hardly fault them for not having used it," Saul replied. "Giving a delinquent child a present is contrary to current practices and theories that are around."

"Oh, is it indeed, Dr. Wasserman? Well, lots of ideas are *around*. The Feingold diet is *around*. Ritalin and Dexedrine are *around*. Behaviorism is *around*. Many opposing ideas are *around*. But from these competing ideas and approaches, people choose the ones that are congenial to them, and then say that these ideas are *around*.

"Is it really a remarkable new idea that these children have to be indulged? I'm not the only one who has talked and written about this. These children have to be indulged for the simple reason that indulgence gives them hope that some other way of living is at least theoretically available to them.

"You say your staff liked Bobby well enough, and they tried to understand what's going on in his head. What's so hard about that? What's going on in his head is 'I don't want to be treated so miserably. I want to be treated well.' "

"We've got lots of mistreated children on the unit, and most don't respond the way Bobby does."

"Thank God!" Dr. B. said. "Otherwise there'd be firesetters all over the place. But you don't even need to know what's going on in this boy's head. The oldest principle is 'Feed the animals.' This is hardly a new idea. I didn't learn it from books. When I was in the German concentration camp, a world-famous animal tamer was put in my barrack.

We became friendly, and I eventually asked him how he learned to control his animals. He told me that when he got a new lion or tiger or panther, he stood outside the cage for a long time studying its habits: for example, watching the tiger pace. But the most important thing he learned about each animal was what it liked to eat. Then he got the food and became the one who fed it, because by feeding the tiger what it wanted, the trainer gained control over it.

"What the trainer said made sense to me. We all know from our immediate experience that we want to be indulged. So tell me. Why do you think some of your staff have the idea that children should not be indulged?"

Accepting Dr. B.'s point was often a struggle for all the seminar participants. Saul may have wanted to argue and defend his staff, but he probably realized that, as usual, Dr. B. was trying to tell him something important. "Look at the details," Dr. B. had said often before. "Observe the process in its most minute form. Reality exists in the details, which is why psychoanalysis is the art of the obvious." All of a sudden Saul realized what Dr. B.'s point was; it was so obvious. "You think it's unconscious hostility to the children?"

"Exactly! You say your staff liked Bobby well enough? Well, how does this liking express itself? I'm very suspicious if somebody says, 'I love this girl very much,' but never gets around to buying her flowers."

"Well, my staff did go out of their way to do special things for this boy," Saul answered. "For example, Bobby seemed to like wood carving, so one staff member spent a lot of time doing wood carving with him. But Bobby acted as if that weren't indulgent."

"Of course not!" Dr. B. said, leaving Saul puzzled again.

But Saul pushed onward: "Well, I thought it would be. I don't know what you're driving at now, and I doubt anyone else in this room knows either."

"Look, Dr. Wasserman. Wood carving is not 'liking' in the

right way, because wood carving is *work*. It's producing something. Even if the staff person views it as indulgence, even if producing something is enjoyable, it is sending a mixed message. I realize it might not be intended as such. But the recipient of the message cannot be sure what the message of doing this activity together is. Wood carving usually involves certain procedures that must be observed—there are rules and learning connected with it. Which is why I doubt that for this kid, wood carving can really be indulgence."

"You may have something there," Saul said. "Because one of the things Bobby said was that he didn't want to have to earn things."

"Well, I paid him off to make sure that my predictions would be realized." Dr. B. joked. "Where would my reputation be otherwise? Always look out for your reputation. Make sure that your predictions come true, even at great expense to yourself. Soothsayers have worked this way since the beginning of time."

Turning serious again, Dr. B. said to Saul. "What can you really offer Bobby at age thirteen? Don't overlook the fact that his mother rejected him. You may know that Freud wrote a bit about the mother's importance as the first love object, particularly for the first-born son. For his own reasons Freud may have overestimated this importance, but the old man was no fool. Can you imagine Freud being voluntarily given up by his mother?"

"He wouldn't have put up with it," Saul joked.

"He wouldn't have had a choice," Dr. B. replied. "That's the point. Being voluntarily given up by your mother would convince any child that he is no good. So, do you want to know what's going on in this child's mind? He's convinced that life is utterly miserable. That is the conviction your staff has to counteract. Maybe *after* they establish a good relationship, wood carving might do it. But that's quite a few steps removed. For such a deprived child, indulgence means that he does not have to perform for the good thing. It just comes. Because of this, I am even a little hesitant about you telling the girl you mentioned, 'When you get upset, take a Lifesaver.' If possible, I would prefer your saying, 'When you are upset, let me know.' Because then it's *you* who gives her the Lifesaver, which makes all the difference.''

"I do that with the girl, and she's come to trust me," Saul said. "But Bobby doesn't trust any adults, including me, which I suppose is what you'd expect, given his experience. But his reaction can be startling. When the staff tried to restrict him, he got furious. I asked him about that, and you know what he said? He said he wanted revenge.''

"A most understandable desire," said Dr. B. calmly.

"What do you mean?"

"If you feel you're mistreated, you want revenge. You might decide it's not workable or too risky, but I think it's part of human nature to want revenge."

"Well, then," Saul said, "the question is: How can you live with a child who sees enemies everywhere and is hell-bent on getting revenge?"

"By realizing that you would want revenge too," Dr. B. replied. "Everything else is easy. Your staff has trouble living with this boy because they see him as a monstrous, completely asocial individual who will never adjust to society. It's difficult for the staff to realize that all human beings, including the staff themselves, share similar feelings and reactions. Once they can say, 'He's just like me and, given the same predicament, I would want revenge too,' they'll be able to live with him.''

"It still leaves you with a difficult problem. How can you safely live with someone who seeks revenge?"

"That's no problem," Dr. B. said emphatically. "You look skeptical, Dr. Wasserman. But it's true. After you've put yourself in his shoes many times, you'll become convinced. When you say, 'You *must* not set fires!' you're at cross-purposes with the boy. When you say, 'Well, of course! It's most natural that you want to set a fire,' it takes the wind out of his sails. Now, of course, you don't want him to do it. It would be insanity to encourage him to set fires. But that doesn't mean that you can't say, 'If I were in your situation, I would want to set fires too, but I know that it wouldn't pay off for me to really do it.' "

"A concrete example would really help me understand what you're proposing," Saul said. "For example, let's say Bobby is with a group of two or three other children. I come down the hall. He wants to tell me something, but another child who also is looking forward to seeing me gets in his way. Bobby cocks his fist back. Then a staff person sees this and just tries to separate Bobby a little bit to make sure he doesn't slug the other child . . ."

"I want to ask you something," Dr. B. took off his glasses and thought. This was a mannerism I saw him engage in regularly: taking his glasses off, thinking, then putting them back on. One day he told me why he did this. "You know," he said. "In *Oedipus Rex*, Oedipus blinds himself partly be- cause he wants to be a seer like Tiresias. The idea is that only by giving up your sight can you gain insight. It's very strange when I apply that to myself. Even though I'm very near- sighted, I take off my glasses and see very little. A few years ago I realized why I do it. Because when I can't see, I am much more concentrated on my hearing and on what goes on inside me, like Oedipus who wants Tiresias' talent."

Now he rapped the table with his knuckles, as if he had just found the answer. "Imagine a bottle-fed girl starts to cry, Dr. Wasserman. The mother thinks she is hungry. What does what we might call 'the good-enough mother' do?"

"She carries the child to the fridge, opens the door, and says, 'I have your bottle right here.' "

"That's right," Dr. B. said, putting his glasses back on. "And pretty soon when the child is crying, the minute the mother heads toward the fridge the child will know the bottle is coming, and so will learn to stop crying so intensely. That is, the good-enough mother knows that waiting is very frustrating and that she has to do her very best to abort the frustration. Knowing that, what can you say to this boy when he lifts his fist?"

Saul was beginning to see his point. " 'It's so good to see you, Bobby. I'm going to talk with you in two minutes.' "

"You're on the right track," Dr. B. answered. "But for Bobby even two minutes is too long to wait. Why frustrate him when having to wait already has him so agitated? Why not say, 'I'll be right there. Just give me a second.' I would interfere with him physically only if I thought he's a wild animal about to lash out no matter what I said or did to appease him. When I think he's a reasonable human being, accessible to argument, I act differently. He knows this almost instinctively.

"So in the situation you describe, if the boy hits, he actually may be living up to your staff member's low opinion of him, even if that opinion is only implied. Take the example of the mother and the bottle. Would the hungry child stop crying as quickly if the mother grew irritated and yelled, 'Why are you crying? I'm running as fast as I can.' "

Dr. B. saw the look in Saul's eyes and asked, "What's the trouble?"

"I'm trying to imagine how the ward would function if we treated Bobby that way," Saul answered.

"I can't tell you. But regardless of the outcome, you feel so much better about yourself when you do what you think is the right thing. That alone is worth the risk.

"It's impossible to imagine what it would be like living under those circumstances because it's similar to a good chess game. While the game allows unlimited variations, every move actually permits only one intelligent countermove. Similarly, in treating this boy, you can plan only for the next countermove. But many therapists believe—and certainly every health insurance company that insures children in psychiatric hospitals these days today insists—that the staff can make a treatment plan right at the beginning. Every chess master knows that only an idiot or a megalomaniac believes he can plan out the whole game in advance. Why? Because every move creates an entirely new situation."

"There's no way I could entirely avoid frustrating him," Saul said.

"Of course not. Nothing works perfectly. And these children have an uncanny ability to evoke our hostility. But knowing that evoking our hostility is their stock-in-trade, so to speak, reduces our need to become hostile. After all, we can't cure this boy overnight. We can only ameliorate his condition. When your staff member sees Bobby make a fist, he can assume the boy's going to slug the other child, or he can assume the boy's not going to slug the other child. When he assumes that Bobby is going to slug the other child, he gives the boy an incentive to do so. When he thinks Bobby isn't going to slug the other child, he gives Bobby a disincentive to do so. That's all any staff member can do. The boy still might hit the other child."

"Wait a minute," Gina said. "You lost me."

"Our unconscious responds to another person's subconscious much more instantaneously and directly than to his rationality. The most I can do to decrease the likelihood that this boy will strike out is to be convinced that if I do the right thing, he'll respond positively. However, he still may hit. Unfortunately, we deal with likelihoods, not certainties. Certainty we leave to those who give the Feingold diet. They are true believers."

"What do you have against true believers?" Gina said.

"They worry me. In my experience, people who know THE right answer always end up burning other people at the stake."

Dr. B. continued. "The problem in our field is not to know

THE right answer. Answers are a dime a dozen. The bookshelves are full of books with answers. The problem in our field is to ask the right questions. That's much more difficult."

"But the approach to child abuse today often is different from the one we are discussing," I said. "It is legalistic, asking explicitly or implicitly, who deserves to be punished for what damages. It often is not psychological. It doesn't ask often enough how living in an abused family affects the child's view of the world, why some abused children invite abuse later in their lives, or why blaming themselves for the abuse makes them feel safer. And because the focus is on how terrible the abuse is, less attention is paid to how to improve the way the abused child learns to interact. Saul and I have spent a lot of time thinking about that. I'd like to hear more about Bobby's personality and behavior, so we can focus on these psychological phenomena and how to approach them therapeutically."

Saul began, "One of the interesting things about Bobby is the way he forms his own judgments . . ."

"Don't we all?" Dr. B. said.

"But Bobby's more autonomous than other children."

"Look." Dr. B. took off his glasses, laid them on the table, and rubbed his eyes. "While the very deprived child is difficult to work with, in many ways he is the easiest treatment problem and the best treatment risk. Because there can't be any doubt about the prescription. All you have to know is to indulge him. The trouble is that you can never be sure how much of this medication will be required. It might take years of such indulgence."

"When you say deprived, I assume you also include severely physically abused," I said. "In many ways the physically abused child is much easier to deal with than the psychologically abused because psychological abuse does harm in much more subtle layers of the personality. If you want to convince an abused child that no more physical abuse will take place, you just have to make sure that he is not beaten up by your staff. Convincing the child that no psychological abuse will take place is much harder. When Saul's staff member assumes, perhaps incorrectly, that in the next moment Bobby is going to strike another child, it is a psychological abuse. And that's very hard to avoid."

"I don't like admitting this," Saul said. "But I once saw an abused kid whose parents had broken several of his bones. I was sympathetic with the boy and furious at the parents. But after some time on the unit, this kid annoyed me so badly that the thought flashed through my mind, 'I'd like to break that little bastard's arm myself!' Over the years I've developed some ideas about where those feelings came from. But I'm curious to hear why you think these kids evoke our hostility, Dr. B."

"Because they approach us with the lowest possible opinion of us," Dr. B. replied. "With the idea 'You're a monster who is going to mistreat me.' That is such a blow to our narcissism, that without recognizing or knowing why, we become hostile."

"I saw a case that was a little different," Jason said. "The father had been abused. When his own son was an infant, this father was so infuriated by his son's crying that he had to put the boy in his crib and shut the door. He was afraid that if he didn't, he might strike the boy and re-create his own past exactly. He struggles with this tendency."

"That man's having to exercise self-control—his struggling and not lashing out—may be better for him and for his son than anything else," I said. "Because in the struggle and the self-control he convinces himself and demonstrates to his son that powerful, destructive impulses can be stopped from dominating and ruining their lives. The effort he makes bears fruit and allows him to live more comfortably with the people he loves."

Finally, we were all on the same wavelength. There was a

brief silence, and I continued: "We argue that physically abused children are easier to treat than grossly neglected ones. I've explained it by saying that we are all social animals. Physically abused kids at least have some relationship with their parents, however deranged. Whereas neglected children lack any such personal relationship, which leaves them utterly alone and abandoned. To put it another way, the physically abused child at least has some value, the value of being the object of aggression. Total neglect means he lacks any kind of value to anyone.

It's interesting. We have to learn these things the hard way," Dr. B. said. "Some psychologically primitive people just know them instinctively. One of the favorite expressions of degradation used by the Nazi SS was 'I'm not going to shoot you. You're not worth the cost of a bullet.' These very primitive, very uneducated people somehow knew that the most virulent, destructive kind of psychological abuse to the person is 'You're not even worth my spending anything of value on killing you.' "

The mention of concentration camps subdued the group and made it uneasy. The room's silence became palpable. Then Saul returned to his earlier question: "So how do you handle the wish for revenge?"

"You mean the Wasserman family's good upbringing prevents you from thinking, 'Boy, would I like to get even with that guy,' " Dr. B. said.

"No!" Saul had to chuckle. "I've shot, mauled, sliced, and run over the 'fiends' in my fantasies. I can accept and understand Bobby's desires for vengeance, but I don't want to become his target. And if I do become his target, I'd at least like to make the situation therapeutic. When Bobby gets hostile, it always starts with someone saying 'no' to him."

Dr. B. nodded. "Staff members should avoid saying no to these children, however difficult that may be. Why shouldn't they say no when the boy has given them every reason to say it? Because 'one straw can break the camel's back.' There's nothing wrong with saying no; it is not such a harsh thing. But for *this* child it may just be too much; it may very well be that last straw."

"My problem is not what to tell the staff. The problem is what to tell the other children."

"Yes! That's much more difficult. The only answer you can give, which they will not easily accept for a long time, is 'We give every one of you what we think you need most.' Then you have to live up to your promise."

"Do you think it's easier to treat middle-class kids who have been abused, since they have not been so thoroughly deprived?" Michael asked.

"Not at all," Dr. B. replied. "In my experience, it is much easier to help lower-class children because they value some of the basics that inpatient treatment offers them: good food and regular meals, toys and good physical care. Since these children appreciate such tangible benefits, they can use them as a basis on which to more easily form a positive relationship to the staff providing them.

"On the other hand, middle-class children take such amenities for granted; therefore, it is much harder to convince them that the staff has good will towards them. While lower-class children are often severely mistreated, the mistreatment from which middle-class children suffer is often more subtle psychological abuse. Furthermore, lower-class children can soon understand, if they do not already know it, that their parents have mistreated them in part because their own lives are so miserable. Since the children have been suffering from the hardships of poverty, they can realize that their parents have been suffering also. But middle-class children know that their parents *cannot* be excused for such reasons when they deprive their children; when such parents pay no attention to their child's real and psychological needs, it is not because of the press of external conditions.

"But I want to add that the hardest children to treat are those whose families live in an edifice of lies, because in them a child never knows what to trust and what not to trust. A consistently rejecting mother is easier to live with than one who is inconsistent. Because if she is consistently rejecting, pretty soon, if you're halfway intelligent, you know you have to get the hell out of there. But let's say she is inconsistent and an alcoholic. You don't know how she'll be when she is drunk. She might be very tearful and create, or provoke, a situation that makes you, the child, strike out at her. And that will make her the suffering victim rather than an aggressor.

"But let's get back to Bobby's situation. Tell me, Dr. Wasserman," Dr. B. leaned back in his chair. "It seems to me that this is such a simple case. Why did you present it?"

"Simple?" The frustration in Saul's voice was palpable. "You think it's such a simple case? Maybe easy for you to say. But every time a child busts a window, we have to struggle with maintenance to get it fixed, or I get a call from administration. Do you really think it's simple?"

"Theoretically, yes. Now practically, I didn't say that."

Dr. B. was pushing Saul to trust his own instincts. Saul finally said, "I think you're right in a way, and I . . ."

"The only thing I don't like about that statement," Dr. B. lifted his eyebrows at Saul, "is this 'in a way.' "

Saul laughed and said, "Sure my job is easy theoretically, but just you try to be a good father to twenty-six emotionally starved children. These kids identify me as the benevolent parent. Even though Bobby doesn't trust adults, he did say that he had a warm spot for his grandmother, who had given him presents. Today he turned around and called me 'grandfather.' Sure it was a slip on his part, but I felt like I've given him his first real experience with a benevolent parent. Medi-Cal will let me keep Bobby only another month, maybe two if I press them hard enough. I don't feel good building that kind of delicate relationship, then having to end it, and maybe having Bobby slip back to where he was before."

"Of course, you would like it to last longer," Dr. B. said, "and it would be best for Bobby if it could last for years. Still, what stays with all of us are the positive memories we carry within. What you can do in two or three months is to instill in this boy some hope that never before existed in him: the hope that somewhere out there *even for him* there is the possibility of something better, of someone who is good to him. You might say that your goal is to find the home for him that he deserves. Your saying 'deserves' is very important because he doesn't believe he deserves it. To create that hope is why you should indulge Bobby."

"Otherwise, you'd never say hello because you'll have to say good-bye," Saul said. "When you look at what these kids lived through, their behavior makes a lot of sense."

"Surprise!" Dr. B. nodded. "Of course their behavior makes good sense. If it didn't, we couldn't treat them."

Not everyone in the room agreed. Bill spoke up. "Do you see a difference between indulging this boy and letting him have whatever he wants?"

"I personally prefer to be indulged," Dr. B. said. "And you know, I have this crazy idea that I'm just like other people. What difference do you see between letting people have what they want and indulging them?"

"I see no difference other than semantics," Bill said grinning.

"Come on, my friend. The difference is quite striking. When you are indulged, you feel you've received something extra. Not giving this little extra is exactly what is so wrong with our care for the poor. At best, we give them what they need just to get by. You can do very little with what you need. Because we don't indulge the poor, we don't alter their view of the world for the better. It's the little extras that make life worth living. Isn't that really what we've been talking about? The little extras—for instance, that tank in the bag of toy soldiers.

"Let's look at that particular situation. Assume no tank was there. After all, no one guaranteed there would be. What inner reactions are possible when the child complains that there is no tank? Many parents respond with 'Look at all I have given you, you ungrateful so-and-so!'

"This comment, whether it is only thought or is actually said out loud, makes the child feel that his parent has a very low opinion of him and disapproves of him severely. The child's experience of this parental attitude vitiates all the good that being given the present may have done.

"But if the parent says—and means it—'Oh, I am sorry there was no tank in this package. Had I known that it was important to you that the set included a tank, I'd have checked it,' then the parent is giving the child and his response a respectful hearing. Then it isn't even all that important that you add that you will get him the tank he wants so much the next time. Why? Because under these circumstances the child feels, 'My parent understands my wishes and doesn't disapprove of them, so he thinks I am a reasonable child.' With this, the child is satisfied.

"A terribly deprived child such as Bobby needs more. He may well need the promise that he will be given the tank soon, simply because all his past deprivations have made it very hard for him to believe in our good will unless he is given tangible evidence of it, something he can hold on to. Witness the insecure child who has to hold on to his teddy bear day and night, while the secure child is well-satisfied knowing his teddy is somewhere around, to be gotten hold of when he wants and needs it."

"But a kid certainly can't have everything he wants," Bill interjected.

"I'm just trying to demonstrate by means of this simple everyday example how our inner attitude makes all the difference," Dr. B. replied.

"You said you want to do something extra," Bill insisted. "What if the child asks you for matches?"

"What's wrong with matches? They're given away freely all over the place."

"What if the child asks you for a flamethrower?" Bill challenged.

"Well, I don't know where you get flamethrowers." Dr. B. said.

"They're advertised in *Soldier of Fortune* magazine," Bill said.

"It's not on my regular reading list," Dr. B. replied.

"Is there anything you would deny the child in your program of indulgence?"

Dr. B. chuckled. "Well, I wouldn't give him a stick of dynamite with the matches."

When Bill next spoke, his voice was serious, as if he were finally asking the question he had in mind. "Isn't it necessary for indulgence to have some boundary?"

"I don't know," Dr. B. answered softly, as if it were sad that the world, especially including a man who planned to be a child psychotherapist, was so reluctant to indulge children, even a child so terribly deprived as Bobby was.

Bill, in his insistence, seemed to want to carry the principle that one needs to indulge deprived children to absurd lengths, so as to invalidate it at all costs.

Gina attempted to continue the discussion by rephrasing Bill's question. "What Bill's trying to say is, 'How far does indulgence go?' "

"It's easy to concentrate on limits and to miss the indulgence," I replied. "It's self-evident that you're not going to give a child a flamethrower or stick of dynamite, with or without matches. But why start a psychotherapeutic relationship with a very deprived child worrying about how far is too far? Saul is giving a deprived twelve-year-old a pack of Lifesavers. You can go miles down that line of indulgence before you reach a border where the signs say 'No further.' And that's the line you must go down to form a relationship with a deprived child. If you get to the point where the child asks for something you cannot give, you have to say something like, 'It's natural that you want that. But I can't give it to you,' and see what the consequences are. A child who values your relationship may react less severely than you fear so as to preserve your relationship."

"You make it sound like all deprived children need is to be given gifts," Bill said.

"No," I replied. "They have to be given the right gifts. Otherwise, a gift can be very offensive or an insult or a bribe. It's not surprising that the very best gifts are things the child wants very much. Although I have treated plenty of enraged children who played that they had a bazooka or machine gun with which they killed all the people who frustrated them, I've never been asked for a flame-thrower or any other lethal weapon as a gift. But I have been asked for toys, candy, stuffed animals, records, and clothes. And when I said some gift was too expensive, kids have backed off in their requests. Any gift is experienced within a relationship. If you have the right relationship, you're going to give the child gifts that are appropriate and will give pleasure. What you are trying to do is to build the relationship and convince the child of the value of relationships. The actual gifts are only a small part of that process."

"What about the girl Saul gave Lifesavers?" Bill said. "Weren't the Lifesavers important?"

"They certainly were," Dr. B. replied. "It showed great ingenuity on Dr. Wasserman's part to select out of all candies available Lifesavers, where the name and form of the candy symbolize that it is intended to serve as a lifeline. Of course, it would be even better if he could be with the girl and speak to her each time she needed a Lifesaver. Basically, though, if Dr. Wasserman and that girl didn't have a positive relationship between them, the girl would have thrown the Lifesavers in his face. The positive relationship always comes first. If it is the right one, the Lifesaver becomes the symbol of that relationship."

"You don't have to have all your needs met to feel you've been treated as special and important," I added. "But there's a widespread fantasy that if you indulge the child, there will be no limit to what the child will want. Give him a finger and he'll want your whole arm. Indulge the child and he'll devour you!"

"Doesn't that happen?" Bill blurted out. "Indulgence spoils children. I've seen kids who were given everything they wanted in terms of cars, bicycles, and even teachers, tutors, and schools."

"What child wants a teacher or tutor?" Dr. B. responded quickly. "Unless their parents have brainwashed them to think they must succeed academically, most children I know think, 'To hell with tutors!' "

"I'll tell you about a real family," Bill went on. "When I was in college in Atlanta I knew a family that is . . ."

"We've all known plenty of crazy families," Dr. B. interrupted. "What does that prove? I've known children whose parents gave them everything money can buy, and yet emotionally, these kids were among the most deprived children I've ever seen."

I picked up the thread. "What matters is the spirit in which the gift is given and the fact that it is part of an ongoing, meaningful relationship, not a bribe to make the parent feel less guilty that they are giving so little of themselves. You can't replace time with you as a parent, with possessions. Also, the gift giving has to be done with the right symbols, like Saul's Lifesavers. Often we can manipulate reality only very little, but we can always select the right symbols."

"I want to be sure I'm clear on something you said before," Saul noted. "When you talked about the kid raising his fist, were you saying that behind that aggressive act was some emptiness?"

"Probably," Dr. B. replied. "People are not aggressive without reason. Aggressive people's motives might not seem reasonable to us, but they're reasonable to them. What I really meant to say is that when we assume the boy is going to hit and therefore stop him in advance of the action, this signals to him that we think he is a vile person. If, on the other hand, we think the child is just so impatient he can't wait, then in our mind he's a human being like you and me."

"But he might do either thing—hit or not hit," Saul said.

"That's right. It's possible he'll really hit. But when you *think* he's just a child who is so tense he can't wait any longer and don't think he's going to hit, you give him the benefit of the doubt and the implicit message 'I think you are just like me.' You have no guarantee that he'll receive the message or respond in line with it. But at least you can send the right message." Dr. B. looked directly at Saul. "Tell us, Dr. Wasserman. What have you gotten from this discussion?"

"I'm very excited to see if what seems so obvious in theory really works in practice. Does it?"

"Yes!" Dr. B. slapped the table and leaned towards Saul. "After all these years I am still surprised by how reliably it works. That's the strange thing. It's strange because our upbringing gave us a vested interest to believe in complications. Deep down we are really quite primitive individuals. Essentially, all we have learned is to delay our gratification somewhat. And Bobby, with his life history, cannot have learned how to accept such delay; therefore, we shouldn't expect it of him. His raised fist is nothing but a physical statement of 'I cannot contain myself when you make me wait.'

"As a matter of fact, I think this boy is an excellent treatment risk. I've known children who, when you say, 'I will give you a present at two o'clock,' will pester you every minute until then. Bobby actually waited the better part of the day to get his present without pestering you."

"Why do you think our upbringing makes it hard for us to see the obvious with these children?" Saul asked.

"Because our all-too-rational thinking interferes with what our unconscious would otherwise tell us. We don't need complicated thoughts to know that here's a child who can't or won't accept delay. Your rational mind and what you have studied tell you, 'It's hatred of the other children, aggression, or a wish to retaliate,' that explain why he wants to hit out. This may be somewhat true, also. But relying on your rationality for interpreting a child's intentions prevents you from seeing the essential element, which is that, like a hungry animal, this child can't or won't tolerate delay."

"Saul is talking about how his anxiety about Bobby interfered with treatment," I said. "He is far from alone. Last week, when Renee presented, we were discussing how easy it is to get anxious about what a child may do. We're all human. What we need to be aware of is that when we confront Bobby, who has such pressing desires combined with a conviction that he will be frustrated, it is our anxiety that influences us more than the child's actions. Also, when I become anxious, my anxiety brings out the worst not only in me, but also in other people."

"You say that we're all human," Renee said. "Doesn't that mean we have a right to be anxious?"

"Of course you have that right," I replied. "We would never tell you, 'Don't be anxious.' All I'm saying is that in our work, many of our spontaneous reactions are counterproductive, and this is particularly true when we are anxious for our own reasons and blame it on the child."

I turned to Jason. "Just as we discussed about Margot last

week, it is easy to be distracted and miss things when we concentrate on our own anxieties. But if we are here to help other people, we have to focus on their anxieties and not on ours, difficult as this may be at times."

Dr. B. spoke to Saul. "Why did you want to present Bobby today?"

"I thought I was right in my treatment approach, but I guess I needed a little reassurance."

"Conviction, my friend. Conviction is what's most needed. Because only your own conviction in the efficacy of your craft can instill trust of you in the patient."

"You make it sound like voodoo," Bill said.

"Well, the good witch doctor is no charlatan," Dr. B. said. "He's somebody who knows his craft, and knows his patients well enough and what they expect of him. Could somebody who restores life, as some of these witch doctors do, be just a charlatan?"

A soft silence filled the room. Then Saul went on. "I've known a few hundred children like Bobby. To me, they're not at all what the world thinks of them."

Dr. B. nodded. "Has it ever occurred to you why the world is in such a mess? Because of the way people think. Now what does 'the world' think about these children? That 'they shouldn't be the way they are.' First we make them this way, and then we tell them they shouldn't be like this."

Saul said, "I think the most common thing people would say about a kid like Bobby is that there should be consequences to his behavior."

"I don't put too much stock in what people say about these children like Bobby," Dr. B. responded. "I look at what they do and who they are and form my own opinions. By and large, if you follow your own opinions, you're more likely to succeed than when you follow what others suggest. Trust your heart. For example, I've never seen Lifesavers mentioned in any article about these children. Lifesavers are too simple for that. Things that go directly into your mouth don't enter directly into a textbook; they have to be turned into an abstract concept first. Then Lifesavers become 'oral supplies,' suitable to be printed in a textbook of psychology or psychiatry."

Dr. B. turned to Bill. "You know, the world divides itself into those who need 'oral supplies' and those who just want to be fed with love. I think psychotherapists divide themselves into three very unlike groups: those who do not even provide the child with 'oral supplies' because they fear such 'indulgence' may spoil the child for life in our society; those who provide the child with 'oral supplies' only when they think this is appropriate; and those who enjoy giving delicious food to a child with love and tender care.

"You all need to decide which of these three groups you will join. But as you do, don't forget that your decision signals to the child what you think of the society into which he will grow up. And if you are convinced that this is basically a depriving society, I do not see why the child should not decide that the only thing to do is to fight it with teeth and claws, as Bobby does.

"What a stroke of genius it was of some public relations man or product designer, a former child himself, to mold candies to be sucked in the shape of lifesavers. Whoever it was, he created a subconscious message. I have often said that all we have to work with are symbols. Isn't that what Dr. Wasserman is doing?

"The girl Dr. Wasserman is giving the Lifesavers to cannot yet swim in the troubled waters of life. If she stayed in CAPI for many years, perhaps the people there would be able to teach her how to swim in them. You certainly don't want her to drown in her own anger and desperation. So Dr. Wasserman throws her a Lifesaver and gives her the idea that 'there are lifesavers to hold on to for dear life, even for me!'

"More than that, Dr. Wasserman can give this girl and

Bobby the memory 'There can be somebody who is nice to me. Not just in my imagination—I really had this experience!' and that memory can become their lifesaver. That's all you can do at the time. To really be healed, these children would have to work through their reactions to their unique personal experiences, to all the miseries that have been their unhappy lot, such as those to which Bobby responds with fire-setting."

"Would Bobby need treatment if Saul found a good family for him to live with?" Renee asked.

"Probably," Dr. B. answered. "A good living situation helps, but it can't take the place of therapy. Without therapy, children like Bobby might not be able to use constructively homes that exist in reality. Therapy might help them to stop being overwhelmed by their chaotic internal life, and it would help them to stop ruining what are basically good family settings with their overwhelming anxiety or anger.

"If Bobby had ever experienced real satisfaction, he would act differently. Because when you feed even the most vicious dog regularly, it becomes attached to you and stops biting you. Genetics dictate whether a dog is an attack dog or a lap dog. But even an attack dog usually doesn't attack the one who feeds him regularly, pets him, and talks to him nicely. In that way these children are like animals, which is why I told you about the lion tamer. So, now that our time is over, Dr. Wasserman, go back to San Jose and to CAPI's children. And never forget: Feed them."

Epilogue

AFTER I LEFT Stanford in 1983, Saul invited Dr. B. to become CAPI's consultant for the next few years. The relationship was quite productive and allowed Saul to further rethink CAPI's efforts and to change its treatment approach. He and I continued our friendship and collaboration long distance. We developed a clinical perspective on treating severely abused children that integrated our clinical experiences and what we were learning about the psychological effects of maltreatment on children with the treatment approach Dr. B. had taught us. Eventually, we coauthored a book on the subjects. *Healing the Heart: A Therapeutic Approach to Abused Children* was published in 1990 by the Child Welfare League of America in Washington, D.C., and is available from them.

Saul deserves to have the last word. I would like to share his comments from a recent letter:

"Early on, Dr. B. remarked that I was naïve, but that there was hope for me. In retrospect, he was right. I learned an enormous amount from him. But at first it was a struggle to face my preconceptions about children and the world. The process has proven to be enormously helpful both for me and for the people I treat.

"To understand the world of the abused child I found I had to confront my anxieties, because they prevented me from accepting and understanding the nature of the child's experience. I had to accept a world with greater cruelty, pain, fear and violence than I ever wanted to face. Understanding that world has left me with a sense of sadness about the way we live and who we are as a species. It also has made me a better clinician and probably a better human being."

The Laziness of the Heart

D AN BERENSON was a classmate of mine at medical school who subsequently also trained in child psychiatry. He ultimately formed a collaborative relationship with another psychiatrist, John Hammond. Both of them favor a biological approach to mental illness—that is, they believe that most, if not all, such illness is caused by biochemical defects and so must be treated primarily by biochemical means. Together, they are studying autism. Dan is in charge of the clinical end of their research; John does the biochemistry.

As a step towards studying pharmacological treatment for autism and for finding a biochemical defect, Dan and John needed to identify clearly delineated subgroups of autistic children—groups similar in their symptoms, because presumably each child would have an underlying biological defect in common with others in that group.

I had lost touch with Dan until I ran into him one day when he was visiting Stanford. He became interested in the Bettelheim seminar and attended it from time to time out of curiosity. He found himself wondering what Dr. B. would say about his research with autistic children and, in the expectation of learning from Dr. B.'s long experience with autism, decided to present a research case to the seminar. As it turned out, the divergent goals of research and psychotherapy became a central issue, resulting in a lively—and sometimes tense—discussion. But at the heart of this discussion was the profound difficulty all of us have in empathizing with deeply disturbed people. Subsequently, Dan, Dr. B., and I engaged in a further exchange of views on the subject matter of this seminar, and some of Dan's remarks and comments from those later conversations have been incorporated retroactively into the discussion as presented below.

DR. B. OPENED the discussion as he turned to Dan. "So what are child psychiatrists interested in autistic children doing these days?"

"John, my partner, is studying their biochemistry," Dan replied. "I am watching autistic children on videotapes, trying to understand what goes on in their minds."

"What do you think goes on in the mind of an autistic child, Dr. Berenson?"

"I think these children are very different one from another. So it is hard to say much about *all* autistic children."

"Very true." Obviously amused, Dr. B. smiled at Dan. "Your answer is a very smart one which commits you to nothing."

"In our study," Dan said, "we are seeing a group of children who are unable to have meaningful relations with other people."

"Unfortunately, quite a few of my acquaintances fall into this very same category, although none of them are autistic." Dr. B. chuckled. "But then you have to realize that I move in academic circles." The group relaxed into easy laughter.

Dan continued with a more serious expression. "To be more precise, the particular boy I'm presenting today has relationships with adults that are, well, peculiar."

"Is 'relationships' the right word?" Dr. B. said. "Using vague, or commonly used, language is apt to distort the observation you are making of these very abnormal children. We might be more correct to speak of the boy's reaction to others, or the absence of any visible reaction on his part."

Dan nodded. "I agree. 'Relationship' has the positive connotation of reciprocity."

"It at least implies a connection," said Dr. B.; "whereas I think one of the most important characteristics of autistic children is their unrelatedness or grossly inappropriate responses compared with what are considered to be normal responses of children."

"Unrelatedness is an understatement," Dan said. "Several categories of emotionally disturbed children seem to have this characteristic of 'unrelatedness,' but so far I have identified only one small subtype whom I would call autistic. I have been studying the strategies some autistic children use to maintain their isolation. I have seen some very violent children lately. The boy I want to talk about today is trying to destroy the environment."

"A child has a pretty hard time destroying the environment singlehandedly," Dr. B. replied with a wry smile. "While man, unfortunately, has managed to damage the environment terribly, even the combined efforts of mankind to date have not succeeded in destroying it. So I do not see how one autistic boy could be so destructive." Dr. B. paused for a moment. "Let's be specific. What exactly was this boy doing?"

"Pulling down the curtains for one thing," Dan replied.

"Well, the curtains are a quite insignificant part of the environment."

"In a research setting, we consider curtains to be part of a room's physical environment. Calling it 'destroying the environment' is simply using, admittedly, some jargon to describe and categorize his behavior."

"I am quite familiar with using circumlocution to avoid being specific," Dr. B. said. "Talleyrand said this more dramatically when he said that language was invented to hide one's true thoughts."

"That's true," said Dan. "But some of these children actually attack people. Take this boy, for example. We have him in a room with his mother, some toys and research objects, and a research assistant who sits in the room with each child to observe them, take notes, but not interact with the child. We just want to see how the boy reacts to the toys and how he interacts with his mother. This boy made no eye contact with this assistant at first. Then, with no warning, he pinched her. He seems to have no reason to do this, since all the assistant has done is sit there quietly. Even though the observers are not supposed to react or retaliate and, in fact, are instructed to ignore the children's actions, some of these children can't let the observers alone. This boy pinched the research assistant, pulled down the curtains while looking in her direction, and then tried to rush out the door. I can't understand his behavior. Did he really want to escape, or was he in some bizarre way trying to initiate contact?"

"I have seen behavior like this many times," Dr. B. said. "It comes about when adults behave like cigar store Indians. Most children will react against a person who acts like a statue, rather than flesh and blood. Such a statue observes nothing, reacts to nothing, and wonders about nothing. And a statue has a great advantage over us. It does not feel, and is congenitally unable to talk."

"That is how many autistic children appear to be!" Dan said with feeling, and then he fell silent.

"I must disagree with you," said Dr. B. "We shouldn't go further with this discussion unless you really wish to explore the subject in depth. You must remember I spent thirty years working with these children. I have published a number of books on my experiences, and thus the topic is deeply important to me."

"Actually, Dr. Bettelheim," replied Dan, "I would like very much to talk about this particular boy because I don't know what to make of his behavior."

"I think your assumptions about this boy stand in your way," Dr. B. said. "Consider your remark that this child pinched the research assistant 'without reason.' We can begin to understand another person's behavior only if we start with the assumption that reasons or motives lie behind his actions, reasons that, unfathomable as they may be to us, seem good to him. To make sense of any behavior, we have to look carefully at each detail and take every feature of the person's behavior seriously. Therefore, if our purpose is to discover what to make of his behavior, a generality like 'destroying the environment' won't do us much good. We ought to ask, 'What might he have been trying to achieve?' and 'Against whom or what might he have been reacting?'

"You know as well as I do the saying that God is in the details. If you describe this boy's behavior and circumstances in as much detail as possible, you will enable us to speculate on why he behaved in this particular way, at this particular place, at this specific moment in the interaction, and against this particular research assistant. But when you say that the boy destroys the environment, I have not the slightest idea what he is actually doing. Of course, if I did not know better, such language might make me feel an aversion to him.

"It makes no difference whether we are talking about research or psychotherapy," Dr. B. continued. "In either case, what the individual *does* is important. If the boy pinches a research assistant or pulls down the curtains, these are moves in the context of some kind of interaction. When we do not know what preceded such moves, we are in a poor position to understand their meaning. It's possible that the child's actions may have originated in something that happened long ago—for example, something that made him deeply distrustful of people or filled him with hostility. Still, since he does not act in line with such an original cause all the time, something in the research situation must have triggered his behavior.

"One difficulty in understanding this child's reaction is that we do not know how he interpreted to himself the situation in which he found himself." Dr. B. stopped for a moment. "What's this boy's name?"

"Luke," Dan replied.

"I doubt that Luke understood your purposes. Most meaningful interactions require that those who engage in them have a pretty good idea of what the interaction is all about: What its purposes are; what end result is expected. But in many interactions between psychiatrist and patient, or child psychiatric researcher and research subject, only the professional knows full well what his purposes are. The more severe the disturbance, the less able is the patient to form a correct idea about such interactions."

I elaborated on Dr. B.'s point. "Let's take as an example the problem of working with paranoid patients. I am sure that people become severely paranoid for many reasons, biological and psychological. And over history, the images paranoid people have used to describe their points of view have changed: Whereas once the devil was pursuing them, now computers are tracking them, and invaders from outer space are influencing their minds. Though the specific images have changed, one thing remains consistent: The paranoid person usually will be convinced that the purpose of most interactions, particularly with people in authority, is to do him in. Yet for his part, the psychiatrist is convinced he wants to help this patient.

"However, quite often the conscious aim of helping the patient is not the only thing that conditions the psychiatrist's interaction with a paranoid patient. Despite his best intentions, the psychiatrist may also feel anxious because he knows that some paranoid patients can be quite dangerous. The paranoid person's behavior may also arouse any remnants of paranoid tendencies that we clinicians have residing deeply hidden within us. Therefore, we have to try to be as fully aware as possible of our unconscious responses to the situation, since these are what the paranoid patient senses unconsciously and is most likely to react to."

"Yes," Dr. B. said. "The paranoid person *a priori* assumes that our purposes are nefarious. Unless we have done our very best to structure the situation to convince him that our true intentions are to help him, his reactions are apt to be based on his conviction that we want to harm him.

"Although many of you know this quite well, since you have had experience with paranoid patients, most clinicians have difficulty extrapolating this to an autistic child, who can recognize even less about our purposes than a paranoid. In general, even emotionally well children have learned that the purposes of adults are often incomprehensible to them. But while normal children of this boy's age have a pretty good idea that doctors are there to help, very disturbed children have no concrete idea about what doctors are for, or what the purpose of a session with a psychiatrist is.

"Let's go back to this research setting. What the autistic child sees is that, in his mother's presence, a silent, nonreacting person sits in the room and seems to ignore him purposefully. What can he possibly make of this? If no effort is made to explain this, any child would feel uneasy. It is enough to arouse whatever little paranoid reactions reside in many of us, me included.

"The assumption seems to be that because autistic children do not *react* in normal ways, they do not care or think at all about what goes on around them. If nothing is explained to them in ways they possibly could understand, or in ways that at least give them the impression that serious efforts are being made to give them a chance to understand, then they feel they are being treated like idiots. This is an insult that would make anyone very angry.

"In my experience, many autistic children are potentially of good, even high intelligence. But whether or not Luke is, and whether or not you agree with me, I still think you do far better treating this boy on the basis of the assumption that he is intelligent. But these are very general remarks. Let's go back to your case and its specifics. So far I know very little about this boy. Please tell us more about him."

"He comes from what we imagine to be a fairly unregulated home," Dan continued. "His father is a member of the Devil's Disciples, an East Coast version of the Hell's Angels in California. The father showed up for a parents' meeting all decked out in leather, chains, and a tattoo. He had a long-striding, macho walk; his black pants had studs up both sides, and he had a beer belly that stuck out below his dirty T-shirt. He wore a leather cap and a black leather jacket with a skull and crossbones on its back. Needless to say, he was a most unlikely person to appear at our medical school! He also was wearing a knife in a case on his belt, I guess just in case he needed protection."

"You have to admit that with his dress the father makes a strong statement about his philosophy," I said. "The defiant behavior and appearance of many motorcycle gang members grow out of their experiences with other authority figures in the past, which makes them suspicious of us. For instance, many of them have had parents who abused them."

"That's probably true," Dan agreed, "and in some ways, the boy is much like his father. He is in a special education program. Neither parent gives a complete description of their child, but from what I have been able to find out, when Luke is home, he plays in the trees with ropes and chains. He spends hours during months when snow does not cover the ground swinging and twirling on trees like Tarzan. I assume his father has chains lying around their backyard and garage to chain up his motorcycle. Mother describes the father as more of a disciplinarian. From what we have seen, the mother puts no restrictions on him."

"As I'm sure you know, twirling is a characteristic indication of autism," Dr. B. said.

"Yes," Dan said. "But what really interests me about this boy and some others like him is the particular way they are unrelated. The only use they seem to have for adults, familiar and unfamiliar, is to have the adult do things for them. For example, as part of our protocol the research assistant brings out a jar with candy inside and a little lock closing the jar. We put the key to the lock on the table. The child can do whatever he wants to get the jar open. Most children in this group take their mothers' hand, as if it were a tool, and put it on the jar to indicate that they want the jar opened. They know that the hand they grasp is capable of opening jars and will use it for that purpose. But that is the extent of their relatedness. This boy won't even look at his mother's face. People are useful to this kid only when he wants something."

Dr. B. shook his head. "Why are you putting a locked candy jar in front of a child, especially a severely emotionally disturbed one?"

"I feel uneasy about it," Dan said, "but as researchers, we are obliged to follow rigorous protocols if we want an experiment to be scientifically valid, even if in doing so we cause the child some slight discomfort. Please understand that I don't like causing this discomfort."

"I'm still perplexed," Dr. B. responded. "Why does your research protocol call for putting a locked candy jar in front of any autistic child and his mother? What makes frustrating the child part of the protocol?"

"Our aim is to see what the child will do to get what he wants. We ask the mother ahead of time what the child would like best, and then we put that into the jar."

"Wait!" Dr. B. said. "You told us that this child uses others to do things for him. Isn't that what you are doing? Using a person, namely the child, to do things for you?"

"I'm not sure I see the connection," Dan said.

"Aren't you using this instrument—the locked jar, as well as the mother—to gain what you want, namely your research observations? Because Luke uses his mother's hand for his purpose, putting it on top of the jar, you say he is unrelated, which he certainly is. But you use the child and his mother for your own purposes, namely for your research data, and you do so without asking his permission. So, by your own criteria, aren't you acting as unrelated as the child does?"

"I don't follow the analogy," Dan said.

"You assume that you are observing something significant about the child: namely, that he uses somebody else as an instrument. But don't you use the child as an instrument to achieve your purposes: namely, data for your research?"

Dan finally nodded. "I guess there is a similarity in that I don't ask his permission to do my study, and he doesn't ask his mother to help him get the candy."

"Exactly. To deliberately place a locked glass jar that contains something we know another person likes in front of him and then to sit and wait to see what happens is hardly a way to relate to the person or to let him know that your intentions are friendly. In this seminar we often speak about forming relationships, how you act toward a new patient as you would toward a new guest you wanted to form a relationship with. Is your action in this research project an invitation to relatedness? If your intentions are good, the least you would do is to open the lock for the child. Since the presence or absence of relatedness is what interests you, you ought not to act in unrelated, or even hostile, ways in the first place. If you do, you ought not to assert that it is the other person who acts in an unrelated or aggressive way."

After a short silence, Dr. B. spoke up again. "Another point about the issue of relatedness occurs to me. You have two sides in this relationship. The way you describe your research assistant's failure to respond to being pinched suggests that she is herself acting as autistically, as unrelated, as does the autistic child."

"Well, as I said, the design calls for the research assistant to just sit there and not to react," said Dan.

"But you don't consider that in some way what you call this child's 'destroying the environment' is his response to your protocol. Is the experiment designed to discover how an autistic child reacts to an adult who acts autistically? I realize that your research assistant only playacts autism, but do you really think that autism ought to be met with autism?"

I expanded on the point. "In Leo Kanner's classic papers on autism, he described how these children treat living people as inanimate objects. On a beach, they walk right over sand, rocks, and people as if all three were the same. In your study, you ask a living person to deliberately act like a rock, which is how we have long known that autistic children usually treat people. Now I know that you're trying to create a neutral research situation where this assistant does not influence your data. But, in a way, your strategy seems like an odd re-creation of how Kanner said autistics treat other people. To the autistic child you're studying, this situation may not appear to be neutral at all."

Dan did not answer as he thought through the issue. When he reviewed this seminar material some years later, he said that he felt that Dr. B.'s commitment to therapeutics impeded his appreciation of what constitutes a good empirical study, and that I simply was reflecting that position. He also felt that even if Dr. B. and I were right—the autistic child actually did see the adult as behaving autistically—an eighteen-minute exposure to such an experience would not harm him. After all, he said, this child and most autistic children spend hours each day in classrooms with other autistic children. The point of the study was to get children to act as autistically as possible so that Dan and John could assess whether the child was truly autistic and, if so, which symptoms of autism he displayed. Eliciting abnormal behavior *was* his goal, since he was trying to determine the presence or absence of a trait.

It was in line with such thoughts that Dan said, "It certainly would not seem the right way to deal *therapeutically* with an autistic child. But we consider this strategy particularly useful for studying their illness."

"That may be so," said Dr. B., "but what bothers me is that you do not consider whether your research assistant's behavior might influence what you and she observe. Haven't we learned that the methods we use to investigate a phenomenon may change what we observe?

"Let me mention a case in point. When Freud wrote *Totem and Taboo*, he based his ideas about society's origins on observations made on primate behavior in the London zoo. There it had been observed that the dominant male in the group denied all other males access to the females in the group. From this, Freud made the assumption that primitive man's behavior was similar, and concluded that society's origin is to be found in a group of brothers getting together and killing the group's dominant male—their father—to gain sexual access to the females.

"Later, when more scientific thinkers, like Lorenz, Tinbergen, and others who followed, studied animals in their natural habitat, it turned out that among the same primate species in the wild, all males had relatively free access to all females. Hence, nondominant males did not experience absolute frustration and had little reason to kill the dominant one. In my mind, this case demonstrates clearly how artificially created situations, such as confining primates into a small space in a zoo, cause exaggerated and artificial reactions. Conclusions based on such artificial reactions are erroneous, relating correctly only to behavior in these exceptional circumstances.

"For this reason I believe that when we wish to understand children's behavior, we have to observe them in their natural environments. Artificially created situations will produce abnormal behavior in even the most normal person, let alone in autistic children, who have so much less capacity to adjust to a strange environment. When you put such children into what to them appears to be a nutty and perhaps hostile situation—providing candies they especially like and putting them into a locked jar in front of them—they can react in nothing but nutty ways. Is your purpose to make these poor children behave even more abnormally than they usually do?"

"Of course not," Dan said, "not in the sense that I feel the continued session might harm them. However, we do want to elicit all the autistic behavior."

"I am not trying to accuse you," Dr. B. said. "Many others are doing similar studies. I simply would like you to think about it more carefully. As you all are well aware, Hippocrates insisted millennia ago that the physician at the least ought not to cause additional damage. I am trying to understand why this supposedly scientifically valid method of investigation carried out by a fine, warm person like you is designed in a way that may cause additional harm, small though it may be."

Everyone was silent, so I now picked up the discussion. "Parents who bring their disturbed children to experimental protocols all expect, or at least hope to get help, whether or not they tell you so outright. Parents of autistic children are desperate. It's a painful diagnosis, and children with this condition are hard to live with. That can break a parent's heart. So parents will do anything if they have even a remote hope it will help their child. I'm sure that you tell parents that your research project will not profit their child directly. And you probably go to great lengths to explain the difference between research and treatment."

Dan nodded.

"But can parents of an autistic child really understand what you tell them? What does a careful explanation of research methods meticulously designed to comply with the standards of the National Institutes of Mental Health or the *Archives of General Psychiatry* mean to parents desperately looking for help for their child?"

"Maybe this father feels that the child's teacher helps his child, and the teacher has spoken positively about our research," Dan replied. "So he brings the child to our study to please the teacher."

"Maybe," Dr. B. replied. "Still, a university medical school is not an environment that Devil's Disciples find congenial. They come to a place like that only if they think they will get help there for something that ails—help which they cannot get anywhere else.

"How many research subjects would you get if you told parents not only that you will do nothing positive for their child, but that the child's inclusion in your project might temporarily increase his disturbance? You probably would get no subjects at all. But at least you would be honest with the parents."

"We do not tell the parents that we are helping the children," Dan answered. "Nor do we tell them that our methods may increase a child's disturbance. Sometimes the children do get upset, but their perturbation doesn't last any longer than the session. I think that our methods are valid because we simply are looking for the presence or absence of particular deviant behaviors. But I agree that no matter what you are looking for, the challenge is to find ways to understand better what these children are thinking without hurting them even momentarily." Dan looked directly at Dr. B. "So what do you think would constitute an ethical research strategy?

Would you recommend that the adults involved act as naturally as possible with the child?"

"Not necessarily naturally," Dr. B. responded, "because unfortunately, some people I know are naturally hostile or exploitative. But I feel strongly that in dealing with unhappy people who come to us for help, or believe that giving help is our purpose, we should act as *constructively* as we know how.

"Any interaction between people requires that they respond to each other. If one person refuses to respond, the interaction is over. When you place a research assistant into the situation, this boy sees her as part of the scenario you have invited him into; he cannot conceptualize that for the purposes of good research design she cannot respond. She is part of the interaction to which the child responds. When, following your instructions, the assistant does not react to being pinched, the child, who expects that his action will produce a response, is very frustrated.

"If any one of us at this table took some action designed to produce a strong response and it failed to have any effect at all, we too would be frustrated and bewildered."

"You might even do something more annoying or destructive so you don't feel totally ineffectual," I said.

"Yes," Dr. B. said. "This child is the same. The situation is probably already incomprehensible to him, since your first action toward him was to put a jar filled with delectable candies in front of him and then leave it locked. Sure his mother would have helped if he requested it, but can you really expect an autistic boy to do that? If his aggressive action elicits no response, the situation becomes even more incomprehensible to him. Being frustrated and unable to elicit a response, the boy reacted in the only way he knew how: He pulled down the curtain and rushed out of the room. Why of all things he pulled down the curtain, I cannot say, but I bet he had reasons."

"Your view is a therapeutic one," Dan replied, "and therapy is a step-by-step process. When something quite unexpected happens, the therapist ought to change his approach. But in research, each study must be clear and separate, so new discoveries can build on existing knowledge."

"This idea of each finding building on previous ones depends on the goal of the research," Dr. B. replied. "But my criticism is more intense. Is this study ethical? In it, you bring a child who, by definition, suffers from a disturbance in his ability to relate, into a situation in which the parents, and maybe even the child, expect that something will happen that will help him. Then, before anything happens, the research assistant declares through her behavior that no matter what happens, she will not relate. Now I know that this sort of setup is routine for researchers working with disturbed children. But it still shocks me. That is why I wish to know what you think of it. Was I able to make myself clear?"

Dan seemed unhappy, as he looked directly at Dr. B. "It is very clear to me."

"What perplexes me is that your research team seems to believe that one can study relatedness, or its absence, through acting unrelated to the research subject," Dr. B. continued. "You also contend that this is a benign, neutral activity. You know that committees dealing with research on human beings have insisted that before we engage in research, we must ensure that the procedures we use are not potentially harmful to the individuals involved, or else the subjects need to be fully warned. Despite this, many behavioral scientists have the erroneous idea that their research is always harmless. Yet an autistic child is put in a frustrating situation, and the parents are not told it may be harmful, albeit temporarily."

"How could I get informed consent from this boy?" Dan asked. "He is an eight year old whose mental age is less than two. The state and social convention agree that parents, as legal guardians, give consent for a minor."

"Naturally," Dr. B. said. "But when a child enters psychotherapy or comes for essential medical treatment, you at least *try* to explain what you will do and why. Yet in this experiment, it seems to me that this boy had the experience —naturally only as vaguely as an autistic child is apt to experience such things—that he was brought into a setting that may push him even deeper into his emotional isolation because people acted in ways that, as his behavior clearly demonstrated, frustrated him even more."

Gina disagreed. "You don't really believe autistic children can perceive that?"

"I do not know what they perceive, Dr. Andretti, or what was going on in this child's mind," Dr. B. replied. "But I am obliged to give him the benefit of the doubt, that is, to assume as much as possible what is most favorable to the child. And therefore, as I said, I would try to explain my procedures to him.

"Lionel Trilling praised psychoanalysis because it required suspension of disbelief. According to Trilling, Freud taught the rest of us to suspend our disbelief—our refusal to believe—that patients, whether neurotic, psychotic, or autistic, act with intelligence or good purpose. I think we ought always to proceed on the assumption that the other person's thoughts and actions are worthy of being considered in the most positive way possible.

"If this is so, then the least we can do is to consider the possibility that the autistic child does perceive what is going on around him in matters that concern him most directly and intimately. This is why I have serious questions about the validity and morality of research methods which are based on a belief that an autistic child does not act purposefully and does not have strong feelings about what is done to him."

"Do you really believe that a kid this disturbed can have his feelings hurt?" Jason said.

At that moment, Dan seemed to grasp what Dr. B. was

driving at. He turned to Jason and said, "He certainly may perceive what is going on as frustrating."

"I am glad you said that," Dr. B. said. "Because while we cannot be absolutely certain about anything with a child like Luke, it is entirely possible that through his experience with you, he had the experience and will conclude that, since he was subjected to such frustrating behavior in a situation in which he might have hoped and expected to meet only positive experiences, the world is even more frustrating to him than he expected and feared."

"I can't agree with your assumptions," Dan said. "I don't think this boy has any perception whatsoever that he might be in a therapeutic situation rather than coming as a subject in a research project. I do nothing to give the child or the parents that idea. Also, I do not accept your idea that even if the boy was so mentally backward that he would not understand the explanation, he might have sensed, however primitively and vaguely, that the effort to inform him was part of a general respect for him as a person. Ultimately, every member of our team hopes that our work will help autistic children and their families. For example, one of our research team's purposes is to see how autistic children are different from retarded children. . . ."

Dr. B. interrupted. "These comparisons never interest me unless I know what purposes the comparison is supposed to serve."

"We hope it will be applicable to educational approaches and school treatment for these children."

Dr. B.'s response surprised us all. "Nobody knows how to treat these children."

"But you yourself have treated some autistic children rather successfully," Dan said in a puzzled tone.

"We did the best we could, Dr. Berenson," Dr. B. replied. "Unfortunately, in quite a few cases, our success was limited. But whatever today's therapists or clinicians do with or for autistic children ought to be built on the little we do know about them. In the very first description of infantile autism, Dr. Kanner stressed that these children have a primary disturbance in their ability to relate. Doesn't it make sense to approach these children on the basis that our foremost task is to reduce this disturbance? We can do it by making all possible efforts to relate to them so that, in their own time, in response, they just might become able to relate to us. This is what we tried to do in treating autistic children at the Orthogenic School, and we succeeded to some degree in all cases. But as I mentioned, in many cases this degree of success was only very limited."

"To me, what Professor Bettelheim says about disturbance of relatedness is hiding behind language," Dan said. "Because to call something 'a disturbance of relatedness' is to use a very abstract concept. What I've been trying to do is to describe and categorize the specific ways these children do things differently. I want to take a large group of children with many different types of evident disturbances, not all of them autism, or 'pervasive developmental delay,' as we call the broad spectrum of such disorders today, and separate out a group of children who may turn out to have a biochemical defect in common."

"What I object to is not that your ultimate objective is to find a biochemical defect," Dr. B. said. "Obviously, we have to explore every possible avenue to find a way to treat these children more successfully. I object to the way you treated Luke when he was your research subject." Dr. B. took off his glasses, rubbed his eyes and sat quietly.

After a moment's silence, Dan said, "You keep bringing up therapeutics. We each have different agendas. I'm just trying to understand him in certain ways without hurting him—and I don't think that what I do hurts him. I sense you are driving at something else."

"I think you get into this situation, Dr. Berenson, because

you do not permit yourself to ask what these examinations do to the patient," Dr. B. replied. "Blocking your perceptions in this manner is the product of your own anxiety. All therapists have to deal with this problem. Anxiety starts right after birth, because no mother can really afford to realize the agonies of the baby in distress—she must distance herself. That's why we all are born and grow up with the conviction that the world is unresponsive to our real needs. The world is responsive to all the superficial things, but when it comes to the real and deepest needs, we are completely alone. Call it 'existential despair,' or whatever fancy name you want to use. It really starts at the very beginning of life, and thereafter we have the experience that the world and other people don't respond to us. They respond to their own anxieties. There you have the 'autistic position.' . . .

"Look," Dr. B. went on. "We could spar in this way for a long time with little purpose. Our time is getting short, which is why I would like to get to what I see as the heart of the matter. I feel these experiments unconsciously mirror our reactions, our inner responses to the terrible rejection with which these children react to the world, very much including us. They also mirror the tremendous anxiety that underlies everything these children do or inhibit themselves from doing. What I am talking about are reactions I experienced myself when I first started to live with an autistic child in Vienna in the 1930s. I was able to overcome them only when, through many months of living on the most intimate terms with this child, I finally developed empathy with her.

"This American girl's mother brought her to Jean Piaget, who said that he did not deal with disturbed children and referred her to Vienna to seek help from Sigmund Freud. He, in turn, referred her to his daughter, Anna, who at the time had just begun to work psychoanalytically with children. When Anna Freud met this little girl, she told the child's mother that child psychoanalysis in the form she was developing it would not be able to help this child. What might help would be the child's living day in and day out, year in and year out, in an environment that was organized according to psychoanalytic principles. After some hesitation, I undertook this project with my first wife, who was involved in Anna Freud's work. To a large degree, it was successful, but only after many months, during which the child was completely unresponsive. I also learned a great deal about this child's disturbance from paying attention to my inner reactions to this girl.

"My first reactions were the same as those I saw years later in staff members when they began to work with autistic children at the Orthogenic School. It took them a long period of spending time with individual autistic children until they could develop empathy with them. After that, their anxious reactions disappeared and were replaced by empathic feelings for the terrible predicament in which these children lived."

Dr. B. paused, looked around the table at the group members, and then continued. "I feel that I can afford to take this group's time in talking about all this because it is our inner reactions to deeply disturbed patients, who completely reject us and the entire world, that skew our behavior when we encounter them, whether as part of a research project or as therapists. Were it not for the deeply unconscious anxiety and sense of rejection which they arouse within us, we would be able to serve them far better than we do today. But we rarely are aware that this is what is going on in our unconscious because consciously we are committed to accepting these children no matter what they do.

"We also wish to distance ourselves and to avoid having direct empathy with autistic children. We want to see them as another species, responding more like apes than like people, for instance. If we consider autistic children people like ourselves, then we recognize the potential danger that we also may be susceptible to falling into autism or may have some autistic element in our makeup. This danger seems so threatening that we wish to deny this possibility entirely. To do so, we behave as if these children were a different species. We do not permit ourselves to think this consciously, but our treatment of them reveals our belief that a generic difference separates us from them.

"Freud's conviction was that all people are alike in most important aspects; he believed that we differ from one another only in matters of degree. His was a radically new view of insanity because all through history, up to his time, the insane were viewed as fundamentally different from so-called normal people. Because of Freud, we have made considerable progress. In most cases, many of us recognize that we have much in common with insane and emotionally troubled people. But when the symptoms of insanity are as severe as they are in autistic children, our society's widespread belief that children in general understand little combines with our wish to protect ourselves against recognizing how much we have in common with them. That is why so many researchers and clinicians assume that these children are unable to respond as we do to what goes on around them.

"The best way to do justice to mentally deranged people, and to treat them as human beings, is to remember the saying, 'There, but for the grace of God, go I.' We must assume that it is quite possible that through some stroke of misfortune, we could have come to act like them.

"We begin to fathom what may go on in an autistic child's mind only if we try, and to some degree succeed, in empathizing with them, asking ourselves, 'How would I feel and react if I were in his situation?' If you mentally project yourself into the research situation this autistic boy reacted to, I think that you too would feel terribly confused and put upon.

"In this connection, it might be worthwhile to remember how psychoanalysis came into being. Before Freud invented the psychoanalytic treatment method, he already knew quite a bit about neuroses and hysterias. However, as far as the treatment of such people were concerned, despite his genius Freud was not getting very far in helping them. Only after he had undergone his own self-analysis, only after he had analyzed his dreams for quite some time, did Freud begin to understand what a patient could experience in psychoanalysis. He became able to fully analyze his patients' dreams only on the basis of learning to analyze his own dreams. His personal experience with resistance and defenses permitted him to empathize with the people he later analyzed, and this made psychoanalysis successful. On the basis of his own experience, Freud insisted that to become a psychoanalyst, one had first to undergo a personal psychoanalysis.

"You often have heard me say that the end of a treatment process often will be determined by what happens in our first interaction with patients. This is why the first thing Dr. Berenson told us about the boy sticks so strongly in my mind, namely that he 'destroys the environment.' This exaggeration of what the boy actually did—tearing down a curtain—can be explained only by unconscious anxiety, which makes us all exaggerate the facts at times to justify our anxiety. Using such terminology also provides an intellectualized category, which helps the researchers control their reactions to the boy's aggression. Of course, they are not conscious of exaggerating the data they observe in this way.

"All this is due not just to the helplessness and anxiety all of us feel in the presence of such terribly disturbed children but also to the utter desperation we feel coming from these children's unconscious, and that we experience as their potentially extreme destructiveness. These children's rejection of the world is tantamount in their minds with its destruction. We experience their rejections and destructive fantasies as actual destructiveness. It all has nothing, or very little, to do with reality; it has everything to do with the unconscious processes we feel going on in the child, and the unconscious reaction this arouses in us. While we are convinced that we are watching the child without any bias, actually our inner reactions distort our impressions of what is going on. This is the overall issue that concerns me and the one I wish to make you aware of."

"This reminds me of what transpired in one of our seminars a few months ago," I said. "We were told that a school complained about a nine-year-old boy who threw rocks on the school playground and almost killed other children. His mother, who understandably was quite upset with him and his behavior, brought him to our outpatient clinic.

"Before we discussed his case in the seminar, no one seemed to have considered whether the school staff's own anxieties forced them to exaggerate grossly the child's actual behavior in a fashion similar to what probably induced Dan to say that this boy was 'destroying the environment.' Only when we questioned what such big heavy rocks were doing on a school playground and wondered how such a little boy could lift them, not to speak of hurling them over distances, did it emerge that what he had thrown was not rocks, but some gravel.

"Now if gravel is thrown, it can do terrible damage, even blind others. But that's rare. Yet what was so interesting in that case was that once we no longer were anxious about that child's supposed 'extreme violence,' we were able to use our empathy more freely, which radically changed the image we had of him and what he actually had done. We no longer imagined a monster possibly murdering innocent bystanders.

"From what we learned about that child, I suspect that he probably did have murderous intentions when he threw the gravel, that we reacted unconsciously to his fantasies and transformed them in our imaginations into reality. In doing so, we had neglected to investigate what actually had happened on the playground and what had triggered the boy's intense anger. I think that 'rage' is one of the major problems patients who come to psychotherapy have. More than just our anxiety distorts our vision of these situations. Much more subtle, unconscious processes also carry us astray. I believe that these are intertwined with our commitment to psychotherapy. Our profession requires that we help people in deep distress, whether we engage in research or in therapy. In research we strive through our findings to help future patients. In therapy, we try to help the individual who has come or been brought in for treatment. We have a deep commitment to our work, which usually is what drew us to this field. When we find ourselves unable to help terribly disturbed individuals like autistic children, it puts our professional abilities into question and confronts us with how limited we are when faced with severe mental illness. Our frustration can arouse our antagonism. And if it does, we can react against the patient who has given us this discomfort by seeing him as worse than he really is."

Dr. B. picked up the conversation. "Overall, Freud had doubts about whether the education required to become a physician was an asset in becoming a psychoanalyst. But he stressed one great advantage that the physician has: Despite all he knows and does, despite his hardest work and most sincere hopes, the physician has the repeated experience that some of his patients nevertheless die. That is, physicians have to learn that even their very best efforts do not always succeed. And because of this training, physicians learn how to remain effective and not let self-doubt overwhelm them.

"Our spontaneous and often unconscious annoyance that autistic children can defeat us as therapists is hard to overcome. So it is hard work not to see the children as worse than they are, justifying in our own eyes our helplessness when dealing with them.

"But let me repeat the facts so we can have in mind what led Dr. Berenson to say that the boy was 'destroying the environment': All this boy actually did was pinch a person whose nonreaction he probably experienced as indifference to his sufferings or perhaps even antagonism or hostility. Then he pulled down a curtain and tried to rush out of the room.

"We cannot assume that an autistic child correctly, and rationally, assesses what is going on. We must assume that he reacts mainly or completely to what goes on in his unconscious and, on this level, responds strongly to unconscious messages from others. This is why I stress that we, as therapists, must carefully monitor our reactions and behavior with such children."

Dan and the group responded to these remarks with what seemed like silent concentration. Finally, Gina broke the silence. "You seem to be asking for something almost impossible—that everybody be so consciously aware of his own attitudes that he won't rub even an autistic child the wrong way."

"Not necessarily," Dr. B. replied, "and I certainly do not expect such sensitivity of everybody, Dr. Andretti. But I do believe that those who choose to work with such children need to be aware of their own reactions. This is, after all, the reason Freud insisted that whoever wants to become a psychoanalyst must first undergo an extensive and intensive personal psychoanalysis. The analyst needs to become familiar with his conscious attitudes and with what goes on in his unconscious."

"I apologize if I am being repetitious," I said. "But this point is crucial whether you say that early personal experiences cause autism, whether you adhere to a purely genetic and biochemical model, or whether you feel as I do that the two interact, but that the biological factors are the crucial soil out of which autism springs. I think that in the fifties, sixties, and seventies, many academic psychiatrists and psychoanalysts underestimated the role organic factors played in severe mental illness. Biological approaches were welcomed because they corrected the overemphasis on environmental, social, and experiential factors. And psychopharmacology gave us new, constructive means of intervention. Unfortunately, I fear that now the pendulum is swinging too far the other way. Many prominent psychiatrists are calling every emotional ailment a biological condition or chemical imbalance. They underestimate the contributions of environment, social factors, and personal experience to psychopathology.

"But whatever mental or emotional illness our patient suffers from, if we let our own anxiety invade and overwhelm us, all our responses will be skewed. What the patient then does or does not do, in large measure will be due to his reaction to our anxiety. And unfortunately, such anxiety on our part will invariably bring out the worst in such patients. Anxiety brings out the worst in almost all human interactions.

"For instance, ask yourself why does a patient become dangerous? The answer often is he becomes dangerous if he feels that the staff fears him. The staff's unconscious anxiety gives the patient the message that we feel that he is a monster. In consequence, out of resentment for our insulting, low opinion of him, he reacts according to the cues he receives from our unconscious and lives up to our expectations. His actions then convince us that our anxiety was justified in the first place, and we remain completely unaware that it was our unacknowledged anxiety that said to him, 'We think that you are the sort of person who is capable of vile behavior,' an attitude that provoked his reaction, for which he clearly possessed the potential. That's what we were talking about last week in Saul's case, Bobby.

"If, on the other hand, we have true empathy with his predicament and sympathy with what motivates him, then our eyes and facial expression will reveal an entirely different reaction and attitude to him. But such sympathy can be hard to come by."

"The autistic child is terrified by the probable rejection he might discover in our faces," Dr. B. said. "Therefore, we must not actively refrain from responding to the hostility, rejection, and even pinching we feel coming from him, as Dr. Berenson said that his research assistant was instructed to do. The autistic child can interpret such total nonreaction only as a rejection of him, or possibly as indicating that the research assistant sees him as monstrous."

"Actually," Dan said, "I forgot to mention that in this particular case, my research assistant eventually did react. When the boy pinched her for the second time, she said, 'Stop! That hurts me!' and pushed the boy away. With this she ended their interaction."

"I do not question that your research assistant had a very natural reaction," Dr. B. said. "But is it appropriate to your purposes and to the situation the child and research assistant are in?"

"No, Dr. Bettelheim. Nor is it intended to be. It shows the child, who, after all, is a research subject in this setting, that you have feelings as much as he might have. It's an honest human reaction to being pinched. You don't say that you like it when you don't."

"It might well be an honest reaction, Dr. Berenson, but I still question whether we can say that it was appropriate. After all, it was you who put the child into a situation that provoked him to pinch the research assistant. She said, 'Stop that!' Okay. But what would you have done if the boy had been able to tell you, 'Why don't you stop this whole procedure. It's upsetting me!' Would you have stopped it?

"Wasn't this boy at least entitled to some statement recognizing that it was the frustrations you exposed him to that provoked him to try to fight back? You say that you approve of the research assistant having human feelings and expressing them. Why not grant this boy the same right? Doesn't he have feelings which he expressed?"

Since neither Dan nor anyone else in the group responded, Dr. B. went on. "Let me give you an example from my own experience. On one occasion, as soon as a psychotic adolescent boy came into my office, he opened the door of a closet and walked in. Since I did not react but quietly accepted what he was doing, he then walked up to my desk, and without saying a word, pulled open the drawers and looked inside each. If that would happen to you, what would you say or do?

"Most psychiatrists would say, 'Come sit down. Let's talk,' or something of that sort, which would not help much. If by chance you knew what the boy was looking for, you could give him an interpretation showing that you understood and appreciated his motives. But this takes better intuition than most psychiatrists have, and more than I could muster at that moment.

"So, not knowing why the boy acted as he did, but still convinced that he had good reasons for doing so, I wished to establish contact with him in a way that would be useful for my purposes. I wanted to show him that I viewed what he was doing positively. So I said, 'You are absolutely right. This is a place to look for hidden things.' This was quite easy for me to say because I believe that is what psychotherapy is about—finding out the reasons hidden behind one's actions, which, strange as these actions may seem, usually make good sense in light of those reasons. In any case, in response to my remark the boy sat down and began to talk.

"What was the magic that produced the desired result? It was the consequence of my remark and inner attitude, which demonstrated to him my conviction that his behavior was goal-directed and had significant meaning under the surface. My comment complimented the boy for his intelligent understanding that psychotherapy is about discovering things which are hidden.

"If you start out with the conviction that an autistic child's behavior has purposes, even though we do not see what these are, you will not just say, 'Stop that! It hurts!' and push him away. Instead, you will also indicate to him that you are convinced that he has good reasons for what he is doing. Does it really take great imagination to realize what would motivate a child to pinch someone?"

Dr. B. looked around at the seminar's participants. "Why might any of you act as this boy did? It seems obvious to me. But you, Dr. Berenson, still are convinced that autistic children act without valid reasons, so that you do not have to ask yourself what the examinations you perform may be doing to the subject of your study."

"Why do you think I have this difficulty, Dr. Bettelheim?" Dan asked.

"For the same reason most people I know have it. When we are confronted with people whose extreme distress would be too painful for us to feel, we become anxious. If you would permit yourself to realize what these depersonalized sessions do to people such as autistic children, who already suffer so severely, just because you *are* a warm, feeling person, you could not go on with this research. So you have to believe that your subjects are not affected and do not respond."

"But, Dr. Bettelheim, some autistic children respond so severely and strongly that I think other factors must be involved. Don't you think biological causes account for why these children react autistically?"

"Well, Sybil Escalona studied infants and came to the conclusion that some of these kids are much more sensitive than normal," said Dr. B. "Most infants are rather placid and begin to respond to the environment only after they have developed at least some mental capacities for understanding it. But others overreact when compared to the rest. They start to respond to the environment before they have acquired the intellectual capacity to understand it, at least to some limited degree. Here, if you like, you have a genetic or constitutional explanation for autism."

"I see what Escalona described in some children in my

research," Dan said, "but others seem to have a much stronger organic basis for their failure to process perceptual stimuli. Two very different types of children seem to be described as psychotic or autistic. One group is retarded. These kids just withdraw because they cannot organize stimuli they perceive. Another group is very hypersensitive and maybe intelligent."

"I believe that many, if not most, autistic children are potentially quite intelligent," Dr. B. said. "Unfortunately, they set their intelligence to screwy uses."

"Some children I see are very sensitive to minor stimuli but may withdraw because to organize what they feel would be too painful," Dan replied. "If I am playing with these kids and drop a block a little bit too loudly, they react dramatically. If a fan in the next room goes on, they startle. Somehow their sensory devices are just turned up more loudly, and I think that they don't have the means to shut things out or to habituate to them."

"My difficulty here is that I am so attuned to working with individuals that thinking about groups doesn't help me in my work," Dr. B. said.

"I'm having the opposite problem," Dan replied. "I agree with your position on individuals, but in my research I'm trying to figure out how one uncovers principles of behavior that hold for more than just one individual."

"Who here wants to be dealt with as a member of a group rather than as an individual?" Dr. B. said.

"No one does," Gina responded promptly.

Dr. B. went on. "If this is so, and it certainly holds true for me, why would you deal with autistic children in ways you would not like to be dealt with yourself? Isn't the only basic principle of ethics in Western philosophy 'Do unto others as you would have others do unto you'?"

Dan frowned and clearly was annoyed. "You keep trying to say that what I am doing is ethically wrong. I just don't agree. Unfortunately, very little helps these children. One reason I think dealing with children who are autistic as groups is valid is, especially with the retarded ones, there is not much you can do to help them."

"Those who have tried to work with retarded children know that you can do a lot to improve their lives, even if the children you serve are seriously feebleminded."

Dan nodded. "I agree fully. Some retarded children can still be happy children."

"That I have not seen." Dr. B. looked around the table. "The happy moron is a figment of the imagination. The feebleminded person is continually frustrated because the world we live in is very complicated, and it takes more intelligence than a retarded person has to live in it well. Intelligent people defensively create the image of the happy moron so we do not have to recognize how terribly difficult life is for these people.

"This reaction is the same one that has led to the widespread belief that blind people have a greater than normal sensitivity to sound. This is not so. Since blind people depend on their sense of hearing more, they develop and refine it. We wish to believe that they have something ahead of us seeing people, so the plight of the blind person will not distress us so. One aspect of the worldwide admiration for Helen Keller can be understood on the basis that her grace and courage permitted us to believe that her handicap was far less severe than it was, allowing us to overlook how terribly impaired she was and how much she suffered in consequence."

"Clinicians try to help retarded people by creating environments where the stressors that frustrate them are minimized, so that they are happier," Dan said.

"No," Dr. B. said. "Less unhappy. There is a great difference between happier and less unhappy. I have known people who did an excellent job working with feebleminded persons. All they tried to do is to reduce the retarded person's frustrations as much as possible. The idea that we can make such deeply unhappy people happy is part of our wish to deny the depth of their unhappiness. Recognizing it would be too painful for us."

"Have you anything to say to a beginning therapist about how to deal with this dynamic, this denial of another person's deep unhappiness and our fear that we may be overwhelmed by it?" Renee asked.

"To be able to work with these very disturbed children successfully," Dr. B. replied, "we have to free ourselves of our anxieties and our wish that these children should not be suffering as much as they are. That is, we have to deal exclusively with their problems, unimpeded by our need to deal at the same time with problems they arouse in us. Of course, I do realize how much easier it is to say this than to do it."

"You've been saying the same thing all the years I have been attending these meetings," Michael said. " 'How do you appreciate someone else's experience?' This is what this seminar gets down to over and over again."

"Yours is one of the kindest ways to tell me that I repeat myself," Dr. B. said, "but you are absolutely correct. I have also stressed something else over and over again. We all are so self-centered and egotistical that, if we want to be good therapists, we have to work hard to conquer these self-centered tendencies."

"The hard part is to learn to place yourself into someone else's mind and heart," Renee continued. "How do you do it?"

"You struggle long and hard," Dr. B. replied. "In spite of the difficulty, you keep on trying. If you try long enough and profit when your patients show you where you have failed in your efforts, slowly you become better at it. But in this particular case of Dr. Berenson's, even though it is a research case, is it really so hard to understand how a child must feel when he pulls down a curtain and repeatedly pinches a person who silently observes him? What would someone have to do to get you to pull down a curtain, or at least make you feel like doing so? That is all you have to tell me."

Dan, who had been listening intently, now said something that surprised us all. "For one thing, the curtains were the only 'adult' object in the room. The rest of the room was furnished only with toys. For another thing, the curtain was almost fully drawn but actually masked a mirror, behind which people were observing the child and his interactions."

For a moment, we were all silent. A few seminar participants looked surprised. Then Dr. B. said, "I knew, or at least felt instinctively, that this curtain had to be extremely offensive to the child. What I did not know was *why*. I am not going to assume that the boy was so intelligent and observant that he guessed he was being watched through this mirror, although often children in clinic settings are familiar with such details, from having been shown them. For this, I would have had to know the research setting and more of the boy's background. Although I was ignorant about all this, nothing could deter me from my conviction that when an autistic child pinches people and pulls down curtains, we must have given him reasons."

"There are at least two reasons I can see as to why he would do it," Bill said. "You might tear down the curtain because you are angry, and that elicits a reaction from the adults in the room, or you may do it because you are curious about what is on the other side."

"If you are curious about what is on the other side," Dr. B. said, "You don't tear the curtain down. You pull it aside."

Dan was shaking his head. "I am not so sure. What exactly the child does depends to a large extent on the child's understanding of people and spatial relations."

Dr. B. sat quietly for a moment. He took off his glasses and closed his eyes. After a time he put his glasses back on and said, "From what you say, it seems to me that you still view the child as if he belonged to a different species. The important issue here is not the specific cause of his behavior, but my conviction that the child reacted to something being very offensive to him. Why was I so convinced? Because I am convinced that these children are not all that different from you and me."

"Most clinicians feel that people act in this way because their biological problem translates into a brain that has aberrant wiring," Dan said. "Therefore the person reacts in ways that are quite alien to you and me. Most contemporary researchers and clinicians today would agree with me about autism."

"That's true," said Renee looking worried. "But I'm curious about something else. You know yourself well, Dr. B. If I am not as knowledgeable about myself, I must view autistic children as different."

"That is not necessarily true," Dr. B. said. "If you say to yourself, 'I would never pull down a curtain, or feel like doing it. I am much too well-behaved for that,' then you will be unable to learn from what the boy did. Learning to understand others begins with oneself, asking yourself, 'What would prompt me to wish to pull down the curtain?' Then the answer will be obvious. 'When I am furious about something that is, in some way, connected with this curtain.' "

"This conversation disturbs me," I said. "I am not sure what causes autism, but I am convinced that the biological component plays a very large role. The whole current debate also involves a radically altered terminology. The children who suffer from what we call 'autism' today have a very different disorder than Kanner described, one often combined with gross neurological deficits. Also, the term is now applied to a spectrum of disorders, not to one specific condition. So in some ways we end up talking about apples and oranges, never acknowledging the differences.

"I happen to see autism's etiology more the way Dan does. But even granting that view, what is far more important and unsettling about what we are discussing here is the discussion about the attitude with which we approach another human being. The point Dr. B. is making seems self-evident, yet so contrary to the approach that is becoming fashionable today. He is looking for the meaning in this child's behavior; whereas many clinicians being trained today are being taught a framework that requires that they observe and describe behavior without ascribing any meaning to it at all. This is supposed to give a more objective, scientific point of view, unsullied by the subjectivity that comes in to play when you assume that a stranger's behavior has meaning and try to comprehend it. There is some truth to that viewpoint, but also great limitations.

"Many physicians of my generation specialized in psychiatry because we found humanism in it, what seemed like the last vestige of medicine as a science *and* an art. Psychiatrists have always tried to rule out organic causes for mental conditions. But what separated the psychiatrists who taught me at Harvard from most of my other medical school professors was that they had an ability and desire to interact with patients as people; they arrived at many solutions through gaining careful, in-depth understanding of their patients, not primarily by using an array of intrusive procedures and chemical manipulations.

"It is true that in those years too little credence was given to biological factors and, in many centers, to psychopharmacology. But I think that laws of nature that apply to chemistry have only a limited application to the problems of child psychiatry. For the one child in ten thousand who is autistic, biology probably plays a large role in his disturbance. I sometimes wonder whether we spend proportionately so much research time on these children not just because they and their families suffer so profoundly, not just because the biological paradigm is fashionable, but also because if we could find a simple cause, like a defective gene, we wouldn't have to bother ourselves with the more prevalent causes of psychopathology, which are far messier, and which would require far more profound changes in our approaches and commitment to children to affect. I do not want to deny the role developmentally appropriate fantasies play. But I do think that for most disturbed and disturbing children, and there are several hundred of them for each autistic child in America, life experiences—divorce, separation, physical and sexual abuse, neglect, and having to spend years in multiple foster home placements with no sense of belonging anywhere—and the subjective meaning the individual child ascribes to the experience, play a larger role. Those issues can seem so intractable and are so much harder to deal with effectively. Yet as we discussed last week while Saul was speaking about Bobby, we do have ideas about how to be effective, for instance, with abused children. But these approaches are not mathematically precise, help only to a degree and in only some cases, and take a great personal dedication from clinicians and a willingness to live with very disturbed and disturbing children. There is little support for that style of social activism, dedication, and self-sacrifice today.

"Times have changed in psychiatry, in how we view our patients and our role. The field we entered made a person's experience central to our study. In large part, that approach has disappeared, or has been colonized by a new, more distant breed of psychiatrists who seem less sophisticated in their understanding of people and the problems disturbed people in particular encounter in trying to live their lives with some dignity and emotional satisfaction. Yet this new breed promises that, through correcting supposed chemical imbalances, we will have a golden future: better living through biochemistry. I don't know whether psychiatry has improved and become modern, or whether in many training programs we have lost interest in teaching how a psychiatrist ought to converse with a patient or form a therapeutic relationship."

I continued my thought: "So I think the dilemma we have been speaking about today permeates most current, standardized assessment methods used with mentally disturbed patients. Like this research project with Luke, these standardized interviews ignore the major impact the specific interviewer and the very restricted spontaneity he or she is allowed, has on the supposedly neutral observations. In some ways, this dilemma forms a dividing line between the different therapeutic approaches to patients. The empathy that we in this seminar find necessary as a bond between patient and therapist and use as one major diagnostic tool, has more or less been ignored in our new diagnostic manual. Empathy may even be considered an impediment to objectivity. Now psychiatrists are being encouraged to observe patients from on high, as if they were insects on pins, and to categorize their symptoms and fit them into the appropriate diagnostic categories.

"Biochemical researchers will look for molecular-based derangements that will explain entire classes of mental disturbances. I strongly suspect they will find some, and that will be constructive. But great damage is being done in applying this approach to everyday practice. As clinicians we need to also be interested in each patient's uniqueness. The diagnostic manual asks the psychiatrist to focus only on ascertaining which group a patient fits in with. In a way, we are reverting to the mid-nineteenth-century idea of Griesinger, a leading German academic psychiatrist, whose motto was, 'mind diseases are brain diseases.' "

"Perhaps it is cyclical. The contemporary clinicians you refer to also are reverting to attitudes that reigned even before the nineteenth century," Dr. B. said. "Before that time, people were thought to be insane because God willed it, or because the devil inhabited them, which made them alien to the rest of us. So those who dealt with them were called 'alienists.' It took Philippe Pinel, William Tuke, and the other great pioneers in humane treatment for the mentally ill to decide that these people were not 'aliens,' but people like the rest of us.

"Throughout history these children have been treated as an alien, subhuman species. The world literature describes quite a few children with strong autistic symptoms as being wolf children. This designation makes it obvious that human beings have a general wish to believe that these children belong to a subhuman species. I am convinced from Jean-Marc Itard's description that his Wild Boy of Aveyron was autistic. He may have been the first autistic child to be described in detail. What convinces me he was autistic is Itard's description of how he fired a pistol in front of the boy's ears, and the boy showed absolutely no reaction, even though he could hear. Such total inhibition of automatic reactions is a clear sign of infantile autism.

"In the last decades, we seem to have gone back to those old views of mental patients as basically different from the rest of the human race, to distance ourselves from them. Only now, instead of demonic possession, we have made the basics of the difference a behavioral or molecular oddity. They are different because something in their symptomatology or in the biochemistry that underlies their behavior makes them alien to so-called normal beings. This rejects and attacks Freud's view that all human beings array themselves on a continuum without any hard dividing lines. Whatever differences exist between people are only differences of degree."

"The attitude today seems to be 'twisted molecules, twisted minds,' " I said.

"Why do you think that at this point in history the trend is to get away from 'We are all human'?" Jason said.

"I don't know," Dr. B. replied. "It takes great effort to recognize the basic humanity that binds each of us to the other, whatever our differences may be. Maybe after a while, people get tired of this hard work. Once—in the 1830s, if I am not mistaken—a mute young man was found on the streets of a German city. He was given the name Caspar Hauser. It was rumored that he was the heir to a German principality who as a child had been placed in a dungeon and deprived of all human contact, so that another person could inherit the state to which Caspar Hauser was the legitimate heir. Just as Caspar Hauser was beginning to learn to talk and express himself, he was murdered. The assumption was that he was killed so that he could not reveal the crime committed against him and reclaim the principality that rightfully was his.

"Jacob Wasserman, a German novelist who lived earlier in this century, wrote a sensitive novel which he entitled *Caspar Hauser, or The Laziness of the Heart*. After the Second World War, a very interesting German movie was made about Caspar Hauser. The second part of Wasserman's title always fascinated me. That is why I gave my book describing the work of the Orthogenic School the title *A Home for the Heart*. Isn't 'laziness of the heart' the reason most people try to protect themselves against the impact these children have? Isn't that laziness what prevents people from having empathy with these children's terrible suffering?"

"It's more than that," Dan said. "I mean, all of us have somehow to find the middle ground between seeing what the true predicament these children are in is and letting the patient's terror and anxiety immobilize us because we overidentify with it."

"I know that overidentification is a theoretical concept," Dr. B. said. "The trouble is that when dealing with these children, I have heard this concept used far more often than I have seen it in action. By contrast, I have found laziness of the heart to be nearly omnipresent. From living with autistic children in my own home and at the Orthogenic School, I know how great is our tendency to defend ourselves against the anxiety and repugnance these children evoke in us. All I am trying to do is to ask those of you who choose to work with them, to recognize your own understandable defensive reactions and to replace them with a desire to do these children justice.

"Think about how much time it took us today to understand just one detail of this child's behavior. It is hard not to be lazy when understanding takes so much work. We now understand quite well what Dr. Berenson first described as 'destroying the environment.' Although much research and writing today ignores or denies the fact, like the rest of us, the autistic child has a great need to be loved and accepted."

Dr. B. saw a skeptical look on Bill's face. "It is true. Actually, such a child has a much greater need for love and acceptance than we do, yet the autistic child is remarkably ineffective in attaining this goal. Out of our defensive needs we fail to see that ineffectiveness, or to respond to the autistic child's need for love, acceptance, and sympathy."

"We usually think of ineffective in terms of having little effect. And these children certainly do have effects, Dr. Bettelheim," Dan said.

"But the effect comes from inside of you! That's what I was trying to tell you, Dr. Berenson. The most important effect comes out of your own anxiety, not from the child. We turn these children into monsters because we say, 'Nothing but a monster could have such a strong effect on me.' Not true. Not true at all. You decide what a monster is—namely, whoever has a monstrous effect on you."

Dr. B. turned to all of us around the table. "I do not wish to put Dr. Berenson on the spot or sour him on his job. If I did not like him and think so well of him from our prior conversations, I would not go to the trouble of trying to unravel processes that are important, not just in this particular case, or in this particular research project. Also, his honesty as a scientist is evident in his willingness to open himself to criticism from a viewpoint that he knows differs dramatically from the theoretical context of his research.

"Dr. Berenson, I know you are an intelligent, sensitive person, motivated by the most constructive intentions. But in this circumstance, where you are trying to gather scientifically valid information, you have allowed the requirements of science to interfere with your sensitivity." Dr. B. paused for a moment. Then he made one last observation. "I can't help feeling that there would be better uses for your considerable talent."

"Thank you," said Dan. "I think."

SINCE THIS SEMINAR, Dan has continued his research, and he and John Hammond have published papers on their findings. Dan says that Dr. B. did change the way he works with autistic children, though he did not persuade him that he ought to alter his research design. And, despite their differences, Dr. B. and Dan maintained a healthy professional respect for each other, as well as a warm collegial relationship.

The hunt for a biochemical underpinning to infantile autism continues, as it should. Because I do believe that aberrant biological processes underlie autism in some fundamental way, I suspect that one day we will witness a great breakthrough in this line of research. But the situation at present is that new papers come out regularly suggesting that some biochemical defect, such as unusual levels of serotonin, may play a role in autism, or that some drug, such as phenfluoramine, may mitigate its symptoms; and then other studies fail to replicate these first findings. As of this writing, the causes of autism remain a mystery. Children and families still suffer. And regardless of what science ultimately discovers the true causes of autism to be, no matter what roles biochemical and experiential factors respectively turn out to play, one problem may remain inadequately resolved. The laziness of the human heart—our inability to empathize and feel kinship with those children who are severely disturbed, indeed the reason we tend to demonize them—has been, still is, and probably will be with us long after autism's cause is elucidated.

CHAPTER FOUR

Transference and
Countertransference

SANDY SALAURI is a psychiatric social worker
with a keen intellect, an easy smile, and a friendly manner
that quickly induces even shy children to play with her. She
has always liked working with children and was a nursery
school teacher before deciding to become a social worker.

In her second year at social work school, she was placed
at Children's Hospital at Stanford, where she was so well
liked and respected that she was asked to stay on as a junior
staff member in Stanford's outpatient clinic. As a conscien-
tious individual, she wanted to develop her skills as a psychotherapist further and to deepen her understanding of
troubled children before going into private practice. With this
in mind, she began attending the teaching seminar.

Sandy had made several presentations to the seminar before
she told us about Eduardo, a nine-year-old boy she was treating. Even the thought of discussing him made her quite nervous, because, as she told the group, "In his most recent
session, with no reason at all, Eduardo attacked me."

"What exactly did he do?" I asked.

"Out of the clear blue, he ripped my necklace right off my neck."

"I assume that scared you."

"A lot," Sandy replied.

"Why not tell us something about Eduardo, and how your work together had been going before this," I said.

"Okay," Sandy replied, "Eduardo's mother is American, born in Indiana; his father was born into a well-to-do Costa Rican family. They lived in Boston. Just after Eduardo turned three, his parents divorced. His mother moved here to be near her sister and some cousins. His father moved here too, and about two years ago, Eduardo's father's parents moved up to Portola Valley. So now Eduardo has lots of family in the area.

"Even though he was not a happy boy, Eduardo probably would never have been brought to a Stanford's outpatient psychiatric clinic, especially at the age of eight and a half, if his school had not insisted that he needed treatment. Despite tests showing him to be highly intelligent, Eduardo could not learn to read. The reading specialist at school wasn't able to help him, and the team that evaluated him at our clinic diagnosed him as dyslexic. They also felt that Eduardo had serious emotional problems that were contributing to his learning difficulties. So they recommended that he enter psychotherapy. About six months ago I was assigned to his case.

"In the first six months of treatment, Eduardo and I formed what I thought was a good relationship. From the first time we met, he seemed to like coming to sessions. Sure he was tentative for a while, hesitant about doing anything spontaneous. He seemed to be sizing me up. But any intelligent person would size up a new situation before opening up very much. After a month or two he must have decided I was okay because he began to play freely. For the past few months, he has smiled broadly the minute he sees me enter the waiting room to get him, and, until our last session, he always was excited when we went down the corridor to the playroom.

"So, I thought the treatment was going very well until suddenly, last week, with no provocation whatsoever, Eduardo ripped a necklace right off my neck. I still don't know how I should have handled the situation. I was shocked and frightened. If he is that aggressive, what is he going to do next?"

"Without an understanding of why Eduardo became aggressive, you won't be able to develop an effective strategy to deal with it," I said. I looked around at the seminar members. "Let's put some thought into this. How many times have we been inclined to say that some patient acted with no reason? Can you remember one single incident when that really was the case? If we say that this boy's aggression was senseless, we have to say that he is a rabid animal. I'm not sure whether his motivation was hidden or conscious, but I strongly suspect that he had a goal in mind when he became aggressive."

"Yes, but the cases I remember involved adults," Bill said. "I'm queasy about saying that children are rational in the same way. Some kids I've known just strike out because they feel like it."

"That's just not true!" Dr. B. objected. "If you want to do justice to a patient, whether an adult or a child, you have to understand how *he* sees and evaluates the situation and his actions. That holds true for everyone, including criminals. Few thieves see themselves as such. All they see is that they wanted something so desperately that taking it was the most reasonable way to meet their great need. A kid will never say, 'I stole it'; he'll say, 'I wanted it, so I took it!'

"What your comment reflects is the misperception that only adults, not children, have real motivations for doing things. You know from your own experience that it is extremely difficult to step out of your own frame of reference and into another person's. When we become adults, we have great trouble trying to grasp the child's point of view and possible motives. For most people, this seems like a quantum leap."

"The situation Sandy is in is especially hard," I said. "Who could respond calmly to a child who attacked suddenly and physically? We would all be so startled and shocked that we'd probably become engrossed in our own feelings. We'd want to believe that there's no way something we did could have caused such aggression; otherwise we would have to accept some responsibility for it. Perhaps more to the point, when we are attacked, like you, Sandy, we immediately feel anxious that the attack might be repeated and imagine that next time it might be more severe. It's only natural that when we are that worried about our own physical well-being, we focus our entire attention on *what to do*, not on *how to understand.*"

"I already said that Eduardo's attack frightened me," Sandy said, "and the fact that I am walking around scared and uncertain about what he might do in the future bothers me even more! After all, he's just a little boy, and I've liked him a lot, right from the start. I don't know what to do. If Eduardo senses that I am uncertain and notices my fear and distrust interfering with the warmth between us, the psychotherapeutic relationship we've invested six months in developing will be damaged, maybe even destroyed. But I am shaken. I don't want to get hurt."

"If Eduardo's aggression did not follow understandable rules of cause and effect, you'd have reason to assume that rather than remaining isolated, it might 'escalate,'" I said. "That's why we have to understand what caused it."

"The upsetting thing was the way Eduardo suddenly jumped at me," Sandy told the group, "grabbing my necklace and breaking it off. It was just a cheap one made of plastic beads strung together and had no sentimental value, but I don't think that anything I did could have set him off that way."

We all agreed that aggressive behavior had to have some

underlying cause. So we pondered at great length and in considerable depth reasons simple and esoteric, personal, familial, sociological, ethnic, epileptic, electroencephalographic, and otherwise biological that might explain Eduardo's aggressiveness. Did his impulsivity reflect some unspecified biological defect in emotional "regulation?" Sandy thought not, although Bill thought that was at least remotely possible and felt he wanted to point out once again that psychoanalysts underestimate the likelihood that biological factors play a large role in mental illness. Did Eduardo have an episodic dyscontrol syndrome linked to temporal lobe epilepsy? It seemed unlikely, since his electroencephalogram was normal. Were aggression and violence everyday events in his home? Was violence an element of his parents' subcultures? That did seem to be a factor. Did Sandy act in a way that reminded him of another woman who had infuriated him? Sandy could think of no such important person in his life.

This search into Eduardo's past, his family history and his biological makeup was remarkably unproductive. Surprisingly, Sandy could not answer many questions she was asked about a boy she felt she knew well. In presenting other cases, Sandy had been precise about the child, the background, and what had transpired in therapy. Yet today she had to apologize many times for having forgotten some detail or other about Eduardo and his family history. She told a bit about the father's Costa Rican family, about the mother's strict, midwestern upbringing, and mentioned in passing that some incident of serious violence had occurred in Eduardo's family when he was just a toddler. But she knew little about it. It seemed Sandy was so upset about having been attacked that now when she thought about Eduardo, his aggression was all she could concentrate on.

The group was at an impasse. Then, still searching for what might have triggered the aggression, Dr. B. said to Sandy, "Tell us exactly what transpired during your session with

Eduardo the week before the session in which he attacked you."

"Didn't I tell you?" Sandy answered quickly. "There was no session. I had to cancel the two sessions before last week's because my family and I were on vacation."

It was immediately clear that we had found a reasonable explanation for Eduardo's anger. But Sandy had a hard time accepting it. "That can't be the reason!" she said. "I prepared Eduardo very carefully for my absence. He didn't voice any objection to my going away, because he knew I would be gone for only two weeks. He expressed no doubt about my promise to come back either. To guarantee that he was re-assured, and to bridge the time of my vacation, I airmailed him two postcards from France, so that he would know I had not forgotten him. Then I came back and saw him right on schedule, exactly as I had promised. I even brought him a small present. So how could my absence be the reason he attacked me?"

"Look," Dr. B. said. "It's all there for you to see, but you must learn *how* to see it. We all draw on our personal talents, training and past experience to do it. I studied art history and aesthetics. To do psychoanalytic work well you have to be able to use imagination constructively, to visualize what goes on in the other person, particularly in his unconscious, and to appreciate dreams, which also are visual. And you have to be keen in your observations."

Dr. B. addressed the group at large. "Haven't I often asked you: 'Don't tell me what you make of it. Just tell me what you observed.' You once told us you had been a nursery school teacher. And you're interested in your own inner life. So what have you observed about yourself and this boy?"

Sandy was willing to explore her defensive behavior honestly. "I admit I felt a bit guilty about going on vacation," she said. "I knew that my absence would distress some of the younger kids in particular. But, after all, I'm human too! I have obligations to my family. I grew up in South San Francisco, and the most elegant trip my parents could afford was the rare camping vacation in the Sierras. My husband and I have worked very hard for a long time to get to a position where finally we can afford nice vacations. And our children are just old enough to come with us and to enjoy experiences that we never had as children.

"But I'm too old to kid myself or this group. I have strong feelings when my own analyst goes on vacation. So I really should have an easier time accepting Eduardo's anger." Sandy paused for a moment and seemed reflective. "I actually was so angry at my own analyst over his vacation that I had to repress it. Not just because my anger was intense but also because it shows how dependent I am on him, which doesn't sit well with me. So I guess what you're pointing out is that I had to defend myself against recognizing where Eduardo's anger came from, not simply because his anger frightened me, but because it suggested that he was intensely dependent on me. His dependence and the depth of his feelings frightens me, maybe even more than his aggression.

"If Eduardo is so heavily dependent on me—and maybe some of the other children I treat are too—how am I going to be able to take vacations in the future? If I am eventually going to practice psychotherapy full time, my patients' feelings constantly will be a serious impediment to my personal freedom."

"That's a problem for all of us," I answered. "Being a therapist does limit your freedom. You can't in good conscience go away for six months, leaving your patients in the lurch. If you take the traditional August off, some patients will resent it. But you can't entirely sacrifice your private life, even if that is what a very needy patient wants. Yet you can be alert to your patients' feelings and wishes and allow them to be expressed, and you can acknowledge that in taking a vacation, you are hurting your patients. While that's not your intention, it is the side effect of what you do, and you are the one responsible for causing the pain.

"At times you may have to take an hour here or there during a vacation to phone a patient who is desperate or who needs that contact to remain stable. But in my experience, because my patients know that I will call them from wherever I am if they say it is crucial and feel they can not talk freely to the psychiatrist who is covering in my absence, I rarely get interrupted on vacation. And they feel secure knowing I am committed to their treatment."

No one spoke for a while. Finally, Dr. B. said, "I don't think that we have finished investigating everything about Eduardo's aggressive act."

"What?" Sandy said. "I see it all so clearly now! Eduardo was reacting to my being away. What more is there to say?"

Dr. B. glanced at Sandy and replied, "While the nature of Eduardo's reaction—anger at his therapist deserting him for a limited time—happens so frequently that it could be regarded as nearly ubiquitous, the form his anger took and its intensity warrant further consideration. After all, despite your anger at your own analyst, you didn't attack him physically when he returned from his vacation, did you? And none of your other patients attacked you in this way. While most patients harbor negative feelings against their therapists when the therapist deserts them, however temporarily, only rarely does this lead to more than verbal unpleasantness, if that. So why was Eduardo's reaction so violent?

"Maybe Eduardo's hostility has deeper roots. Could his intense reaction to your absence reflect an earlier trauma? Were there prior desertions that your vacation might have recalled to Eduardo's conscious or unconscious mind?"

"Of course there were!" Sandy said, seeming pleased and excited. "Eduardo's reaction to my absence must have reawakened his anguish about his father's abandoning him when his parents divorced."

Sandy had finally recognized in Eduardo's behavior a classic instance of the phenomenon of *transference*, the patient's re-creations in the therapy sessions of feelings from the past, bringing these feelings to the session in full force, as if they were current events. They show the therapist the emotional by-products of traumas that may have occurred years or decades ago; yet those traumas' effects exist almost unaltered in the patient's unconscious.

"As therapists, it's painful for us to hurt children," I said. "It goes against exactly what we are committed to doing and makes us feel guilty. But if we are aware that we sometimes have to act in our self-interest and that that incidentally may cause our patients pain, we can be more empathic toward parents who can be very hurtful to their children. These parents usually are not the monsters we sometimes imagine them to be. In a large number, though certainly far from all of these cases, the parents do not want to cause suffering, but feel that circumstances beyond their control force them to do so. And many feel guilty for that."

"You know," Sandy said. "I really disliked Eduardo's father when Eduardo's mother first told me how cruel he could be. I felt furious when she told me that one day, with no warning, he had simply picked up and deserted the family. Then came the real shocker. I met the father, and he actually seemed to be a nice man who really cares deeply about Eduardo."

"Isn't it possible," Dr. B. pointed out, "that just as you were convinced that you could not deprive your family of a vacation, Eduardo's father felt compelled to leave his family? In self-protection, he might have been unable or unwilling to recognize emotionally that simultaneously he was inflicting a severe trauma on his son. But even if we recognize that, we can't permit ourselves to be seduced into defending or justifying the father's actions.

"Doing so can be tempting for all of us. Look how easily you were impressed that this father seemed to be a nice, concerned parent. In other clinical situations, a parent's real plight can tempt us to sympathize with the parent against the child. And whether or not the parent has, in a deeper sense, caused a child's difficulties, some children can make life miserable for their parents.

"But we have to side with our patient, the child, who essentially is defenseless against the world of adults. Of course, just as a person's defender in a lawsuit may have to bring to his client's attention (when doing so is to his client's advantage) that he has distorted certain facts of reality, a therapist may have to bring to her patient's attention certain distortions in his view of things, but only when this clearly is to the patient's benefit and to the benefit of his therapy.

"And to get back to your case, however pleasant Eduardo's father may be now, he still deserted his son. Let's say—and I'm being highly speculative just to make a point—that from the father's perspective, Eduardo's mother was such a miserable person to live with that divorcing her seemed his only way out. This wouldn't in the slightest way mitigate the harm to Eduardo. If the father's viewpoint is accurate, it could even increase the trauma, because it left Eduardo alone without a father who could defend him against a very difficult woman.

"Today divorces are so frequent that society readily accepts them. I know quite a few child therapists who are themselves divorced and live apart from their children. For very understandable reasons, these therapists may find it difficult to confront the fact that such desertion causes profound pain to and difficulty for children, including their own. So for personal reasons, they may defend another divorced parent's actions. I recognize that some marriages are so miserable that living under these conditions actually could subject a child to more damage than a divorce. However, most young children can not really conceive that their lives may have been even worse if their parents had not separated. Also, most young children care little about who is the guilty party in a divorce. They know only how badly they suffer from the desertion.

"Therapy is a relationship, an experiment, a test case. And in that mixture, a skilled therapist must avoid projecting her own feelings into the therapeutic relationship. This includes even feelings she harbors strongly, such as that desertions through divorce, or even through a vacation, are unavoidable, so a child just has to accept them. When such understandable feelings creep into a therapeutic relationship, they become what are called technically *countertransference phenomena.* While in themselves the feelings and attitudes the therapist carries are commonplace, they are psychological processes in the therapist that interfere with her ability to function therapeutically. They *must* be denied a place in the therapeutic relationship, because they are detrimental to it."

"Another example of countertransference in Eduardo's case is the anxiety you were having about his aggressive behavior," I added. "I have seen this in many other instances: The very same psychotherapist who can understand and accept destructive behavior, as long as it is directed elsewhere, becomes unable to deal with such behavior when it seems directed against her. Then her own anxiety overwhelms her, and such behavior becomes emotionally unacceptable. While a self-defensive reaction is normal and understandable, this personal reaction diverts the therapist's energy into thinking about how to protect herself against repeated incidents. With such personal reactions intruding, a therapist becomes unable to apply a fundamental lesson of psychotherapy that nobody acts without what *he* considers good reasons."

Dr. B. returned to the issue of Eduardo's desertion. "Your need to defend yourself against recognizing that your vacation hurt Eduardo was based on *your* emotional needs, not on Eduardo's. That's why it was countertransference. That prevented you from comprehending that his intense feelings reflected the fact that no matter how minor and benign any desertion was in reality, to his unconscious mind it was a mirror image of the original desertion by his father."

Dr. B. looked around the seminar table. "Now one detrimental aspect of countertransference phenomena is that they easily can blind the therapist to transference phenomena, those extremely important way stations in the patient's movement toward mental health. And as long as we are discussing transference and countertransference, let's not forget that a patient also can evoke insight in the therapist."

Dr. B. turned to Sandy. "You saw causing Eduardo pain as bad for the therapy. Yet what made it painful was something intrinsic to the psychotherapeutic process—the fact that psychotherapy promotes transference. This pain also is a therapeutic opportunity that shows that his therapy is progressing well. Why? Because old traumas can be worked through in the psychotherapeutic situation only when they are brought into it. So by permitting a faithful reproduction of the original, severe desertion, transference has induced Eduardo to connect it with the present, minor desertion of your vacation. And that is all good for the psychotherapeutic process."

"Let me see if I am following you," Sandy said. "Are you telling me that if my own feelings had not gotten in the way, I might not have seen this as an obstacle to therapy. Instead of frightening me, his aggression might have pleased me because it offered us a chance to work through the original desertion's aftereffects?"

Dr. B. nodded.

"I still don't think I'll ever be delighted to have someone attack me," Sandy said.

"He didn't attack you," I interjected. "He shocked and frightened you. He hurt your feelings, but he didn't hurt you physically. In fact, I suspect that he made sure not to. It's hard to rip a necklace off someone's neck without hurting them. Sure you were alarmed. Who wouldn't be at first? But when you got overwhelmed and began to see Eduardo's aggression as a serious physical attack, you made it a threat to therapy's progress. You didn't see this act as a communication you needed to decode.

"Now you can't let yourself be attacked physically, but you have six months of experience with Eduardo and know what kind of person he is. In keeping with his nature, Eduardo was careful to hurt your feelings and your beads, not your body. He cares about you and seems to know that physical violence is a boundary he can not go beyond. So he is the same boy you've known and liked for the past six months."

"Should Sandy just tolerate his aggressiveness?" Gina asked.

"No," I said. "To tolerate this aggression would be to say to Eduardo, 'You can't hurt me. You are incompetent.' Tolerance is to not take a person seriously. Patients do not want to be tolerated. They want to be reacted to. And if you don't react, the patient has to escalate. If one behavior isn't strong enough to get a response, the child must use stronger ways. Every behavior is goal-directed, and your task as a psychotherapist is not to tolerate, but to understand the child's goal and respond appropriately."

Everyone was silent for a while. Finally, I went on. "For a psychotherapy to proceed correctly, anger and hostility *must* be recovered, relived, and worked through in the transference. Like other aspects of the unconscious, our rage contains enormous energy that can be harnessed to our interests, if it is not repressed and tightly bound up because we fear it so. How to harness this angry energy, this strong, frightening storm, will be an aspect of your future psychotherapeutic work, not just with Eduardo but with many patients and perhaps even with yourself. Fear of this rage leads numerous patients to inhibit and constrain themselves. As the years go by, they become more and more rigid, all the time trying to hide from others, and usually from themselves, how angry and hostile they feel. So, greater and greater parts of their potential are sacrificed in a defensive maneuver. This rage can not be dealt with constructively simply by telling a person that he ought to be honest and blow off steam when and where he feels like it. That can be extremely destructive to relationships and careers. Therapy, however, may be the only place where people really have the opportunity to say and feel whatever they want to without serious repercussions or retaliation.

"Only after these negative feelings have been adequately dealt with in the relationship between therapist and patient, can the positive feelings come to the fore. So only after Eduardo's anger at being deserted has become manifest, and after the hostility this anger provoked can be experienced, explored, and put in some therapeutic context and perspective, can Eduardo recover the love he feels for his father—a love that went underground because his father's desertion so disappointed, disillusioned, and infuriated him.

"I don't know how this will become manifest in the transference. Eduardo's love for his father may first reappear as love for his therapist, you, Sandy. Eduardo's hostility against you can be understood mainly as a transference of anger originally directed against his father, who seems to have played falsely with Eduardo's love, deserting him at a moment when he needed his father so desperately. In the same way, you cannot take these positive feelings as truly belonging to you. They ought to be regarded only as Eduardo's transferring love for his father onto you, his therapist."

"You all know that the unconscious has no awareness of time," Dr. B. went on. "Exactly because neither time, nor space, nor causality organizes our unconscious's content, and because logical contradictions can easily persist in it, the unconscious is chaotic. The 'categories a priori' which Kant established as ruling all that goes on in our mind refer, of course, only to our conscious or rational mind. This timelessness makes it possible for psychoanalysis to proceed and succeed, for it permits the patient to reexperience past events in the transference as if they were present experiences, with a form and intensity they possessed when they were fresh wounds. It allows the patient to work through such past events in the present. And as far as the unconscious is concerned, this working through influences the consequences past traumas exert on present feelings and functioning, diminishing the power they exercise in the unconscious. Psychotherapeutic work sometimes transmutes them as if the events had never happened, or had happened in a different form. In some ways, the patient can remake his past through psychotherapy, throwing a new light on it that dispels much of its stubborn, destructive power, at least as far as its impact on the present is concerned.

"Through slowly analyzing himself, the patient succeeds in breaking the unnoticed, unconscious stranglehold his past has on his present. As he separates the two, the past becomes securely that, and it is no longer experienced as if it were the present."

When everyone was silent, I said, "Coming back to Eduardo's behavior, for it to be understood and for its meaning to be fully appreciated, we must remind ourselves of the fact that in the mind of a child, particularly an emotionally disturbed child, past is present and present is past. For a disturbed child, as in the very young normal child, the future is at most this afternoon, and injustices and indignities that happened in the past are expected not only to recur in the present but to dominate it.

"Even though you know this, Sandy, in this situation you were unable to apply this knowledge. Theoretical knowledge can easily become inoperative when applying it threatens to make our lives more difficult, in this case by making it more problematic for you to take vacations.

"But I'm not ready to leave the necklace," I went on. "Can you tell us why Eduardo tore it off?"

"Why are you pestering her?" Bill said. "We've just spent the last hour discussing that question at length. This is ridiculous. What aspect haven't we covered?"

"I still don't understand what Eduardo was trying to say when he pulled the beads from Sandy's neck," I went on. "Every action a child makes is a communication to us. We've come a long way in understanding this one. We no longer say that this was the insane behavior of an impulsive boy who may suffer from a dyscontrol syndrome. We all realize that Eduardo was telling Sandy how upset he was that she had, from his point of view, deserted him.

"What still puzzles me is why, of all the possible ways he had to show his deep hurt, he chose this particular one. After all, he could have torn Sandy's clothing, or broken some object on her desk that he thought she cherished—all things I've seen children do when they were sufficiently disappointed, frustrated, or angry. If Eduardo really had wanted to hurt Sandy physically, he could have hit her, thrown a heavy toy at her, bit her, or pulled her hair. Since he did not, as I said, I suspect his aim was to hurt her feelings.

"Where words are concerned, therapists are well aware that we need to pay careful attention to the specific words, phrases, or vulgarities through which a patient chooses to convey his thoughts. When the patient vents his feelings through actions, it often is harder to decipher the message in the action. In studying to practice child psychotherapy, we learn to communicate in many 'languages' or modes, because children express themselves in different ways at different ages. Thus, a child psychotherapist must be skilled in understanding displacements, the way a child expresses his deepest feeling and concerns in play, projected into dolls or games.

"So we child therapists must learn the meaning of symbols and speak the language of dolls, toys, sports, and games. I remember one trainee who conducted almost the entire therapy with a school-aged boy in baseball analogies. While an adult therapist will follow a patient's train of thought and knows that when an adult patient abruptly changes the topic, it is likely to be because he is anxious, when a child changes the flow of play—what we technically call a 'play interruption'—he or she is likely to have become anxious about what was being played out in displacement. Furthermore, the psychotherapist knows that all actions in therapy are messages that need be decoded and understood regardless of the 'language' the patient uses. That's the essence of a correct interpretation: a message back to the patient that I hear you and understand what you are trying to tell me. But in child therapy, the interpretation usually ought to stay within the displacement, for example, talking about what the toy doll did, not about what the action means in the child patient's own life and family. If we do make a direct interpretation to a child, it can feel very intrusive, make the child anxious, and lead him or her to change the subject."

Dr. B. spoke. "We all expended considerable energy and effort today to understand Eduardo's aggression." He looked at Sandy. "You have been open and inquisitive. It is only human to be attached to the ideas we have because we worked so hard to arrive at them.

"But Freud was well aware that it was very easy to close one's mind to alternatives once we had explained a patient's behavior to our satisfaction. That explanation might overlook a deeper symbolic meaning, which may be why Freud advocated that the psychoanalyst listen to his patients with what he called 'a free-floating attention,' or what Theodor Reik named 'listening with the third ear.' Both terms warn against listening with concentrated attention, focused like a spotlight on the patient's words, because that precludes keeping the mind open to what is on our attention's periphery and to the dimly illuminated outcroppings of one's own unconscious. The therapist has to heed both her conscious reactions to what the patient is saying and her own unconscious reactions to it. Only then can she become reasonably certain of responding fully to *all* that goes on in the patient's mind. That *all* includes what goes on in the patient's conscious mind as well as on different levels of the patient's unconscious, which often operate independently of each other.

"Therefore, if we want to understand better, or more fully, what compelled Eduardo to express his feelings by tearing off Dr. Salauri's necklace or, probably more correctly, what went on in his conscious *and* in his unconscious, which in their combination motivated his aggressive action, we have to free ourselves from considering only the general description of his behavior as an angry act. Let's also pay careful attention to the particular form his aggression took. Since viewing it as 'tearing off the necklace' does not seem to offer any further clues, how else can we think of and describe his action?"

Several seminar members came up with suggestions.

"You could say he wrenched off her chain," Jason said.

"But that would just be making the verb more violent," I replied.

"Maybe Eduardo wanted to punish Sandy by depriving her of her adornments," Gina said.

"Better," Dr. B. replied. "Your comment shows that you are wondering what this act's symbolic goal might have been. You are considering the possibility that Eduardo's act might have been goal-directed, more interested in his action's end result than in the action itself. This suggests that Eduardo might have chosen this particular act because it was uniquely suited to convey some very specific message."

With a gleam in his eye, Dr. B. suggested, "Perhaps Eduardo's goal was only to break the necklace. But to break it, unless he had magical skills, he had to tear it off Sandy's neck to achieve his goal, if this is what it was, thereby seeming aggressive."

"What?" Bill said.

Everyone looked perplexed. "Let your mind wander a bit,

Dr. Salauri," Dr. B. said. "Could Eduardo be giving you some very specific message in tearing this circle, this uninterrupted string of beads."

Sandy was quiet for a moment, then her face lit up. "Yes. Yes, of course. But you gave me a big hint. You're trying to tell me that Eduardo found a way to protest and repay me in kind: a broken chain of beads in repayment for a broken string of sessions."

Dr. B. nodded.

"I think that's pretty farfetched," Jason said.

"To say the least," Bill added.

But Michael was nodding. "I like the idea. It makes sense to me."

"While the idea is elegant, it does sound farfetched to me too," I said. "But the crucial question is not whether this interpretation hits a bull's-eye. What is essential is whether you accept that Eduardo had some precise, not impulsive, reason for selecting the beads out of all the items he could have broken in your office, and recognize that whatever his communication, he was careful not to hurt you physically. Pondering what he had in mind, what he was trying to communicate and achieve, will help move the therapeutic process forward. And if Dr. B.'s hypothesis contributes to that forward motion and deepening understanding between you and Eduardo, it will have been constructive."

"Well I think it's more than that," Sandy said. "Dr. B.'s on to something. I was in the room with Eduardo, and I think it is the logical symbolic meaning of his action."

"Then use it in your work with him," I said. "After all, your goal is to foster the ongoing therapeutic conversation between Eduardo and you. In therapy, that conversation needs to be from the unconscious to the unconscious at some times. Each patient and therapist develop their own 'language' to speak this way, which probably is why patients in Freudian analysis have Freudian dreams and those in Jungian analysis have Jungian dreams. Both are ways to communicate the unconscious contents in an agreed-upon language.

"But something else about Eduardo's aggression is important. In another sense, what he did actually was a very positive step forward. A while ago you said that 'out of the clear blue' Eduardo pulled off your necklace. But you also said today that his father had left 'with no warning.' Perhaps like his father's leaving, your vacation made him a passive victim. By breaking your chain of beads, he actively inflicted on you, in a symbolic form, what you made him suffer passively."

These possibilities and insights put the situation and Eduardo's role in it in an entirely new light. What had worried Sandy before now pleased her. A big smile lit up her face. She said, "I knew I liked that boy's spunk!"

"You have a great deal to be pleased with," Dr. B. said. "Your work with Eduardo has borne fruit. When he started psychotherapy with you, he was a boy who could deal with traumas inflicted on him only in a passive, resistant way, like a powerless victim. He refused to learn in school as a way of expressing his unwillingness to come to terms with the world because, he felt, the world refused to come to terms with him. Through his action in therapy with you, he has dared to become active in his own behalf, at least in the therapeutic situation. So, what you originally viewed as an impasse in therapy, if not a threat to its continuing, you now realize was an important step forward in it. In some ways, this is similar to a child's saying 'no' to us. It is very important for us as parents and therapists to accept the child's rejection of us. Individuation and the experience of self-determination occur around the child's 'no.'

"Since we have a little time left in today's seminar," Dr. B. remarked, "I think it would be worthwhile to consider somewhat more generally this issue of a communication's real content in contrast to its symbolic content. We ought to think about that more often in psychotherapeutic situations.

"After all, the psychotherapeutic situation reflects the to-
tality of the patient's life and the therapist's attitude toward
that life. In psychotherapy, whether the patient is a child or
an adult, we are deeply committed to the attitude that we
cannot actively solve real-life problems for the patient. We
can deal with them only on a symbolic level, which we say
is effective. For the last hour we have been talking about
Eduardo and wondering about the message that his action
contained. How often do we reflect on the symbolism implicit
in our own actions as therapists?

"In psychotherapy, we shift back into everyday reality at
the session's end without reflecting on the symbolic meaning
of the sudden switch in mental environments. After forty-five
or fifty minutes we say, 'Your time is over,' or 'My time is
over,' or whatever phrase we use. Abruptly, at a point the
clock defines, we who say that the unconscious has no sense
of time, switch from the symbolic to the reality level.

"We have to ask ourselves what that switch symbolizes,
that as a psychotherapist you do not stop sessions at a point
that is logical psychologically, but at one the clock sets. For
forty-five or fifty minutes you, the therapist, deal purely with
symbolism, and then, when it's convenient for you, with very
little consideration given to the fact that you have persuaded
the patient to deal with everything on a symbolic level, you
suddenly move over to the practical world and say to hell
with symbolism.

"Actually, if you look at the symbolic message in this action, it says that what a therapist really wants is for his or
her patients to become compulsive-neurotics, people who
should be absolutely able to isolate things from one another.
That's an issue Freud never really dealt with."

"But Jacques Lacan deals with it extensively," Michael
said.

"That's right," said Dr. B. "Lacan, the great French psychoanalyst, wrote that there's no time in the unconscious, so

a therapy session's length should not be preset in time. This point has a great deal of truth, but of course, think of how impractical your time schedule would be if you didn't assign each patient a preset amount of time for his or her session. How could you manage otherwise?"

"If anything," Gina said, "my difficulty is ending an hour on time, not wanting to end it earlier."

"Well," Dr. B. said, "Freud used a device that really works very well, but which I hardly ever see advocated here. At the end of every session, Freud summarized what had transpired for the patient, and in this way provided closure to the session, a transition from the symbolic to the real life."

"Was it always clear to him what had transpired?" Gina asked. "For me, what was actually happening during a session often becomes clear only hours after it has ended."

"Sure, it's difficult to make these summaries at first. But if you make them systematically over a couple of years, like everything, you learn to do it well. It's true that after any given session you might not be able to summarize the deeper meaning. But you can say something like 'today we covered a great deal of material,' or 'today was slow—why was it so?' Of course, it's preferable, but not always possible, to say what the meaning is."

Gina leaned forward and said enthusiastically, "Yes. It does seem like a natural, important part of any therapy for there to be times when what's happening isn't immediately understandable for either person. Summarizing at the end of such an hour could reassure both the patient and the therapist by reiterating that times like this are part of therapy."

"One other thing was also customary with Vienna psychoanalysts," Dr. B. said. "The analyst ended every hour saying, more or less, 'We are going to continue.' "

"And Freud saw his patients six days a week," I said.

"Yes," Dr. B. went on. "So the analyst gave both a summary and a reminder that there was still unfinished business."

"I've often thought there should be a recovery room on the other end, a place to stop before reentering the real world," Sandy said.

"If a session really was good and got into deep material, the transition out is very difficult for the patient," Dr. B. replied. "Every patient should theoretically allow himself time to readjust. But most patients are scheduled too tightly. Look at children: These days they are so heavily scheduled that after their appointment with you, they immediately have to go to their next activity. So they are picked up and are not allowed this time. But that is characteristic of how our society deals with time.

"Any questions?" Dr. B. said. When the group was silent, he went on. "I hope you all have gained insight into how important it is that we work hard to understand a patient's message. Theoretical knowledge is general. It is very useful, because without it the therapist may never recognize what a patient is suffering from. But for every patient, like for Eduardo, the problem is specific and unique. The great danger is that the therapist, and often the patient, is satisfied when she recognizes what is involved in general, such as that Eduardo was angry at Dr. Salauri. But an entirely different form of information usually is forthcoming if the therapist focuses on a different set of specifics.

"This can be hard, time-consuming work. But if you listen with the 'third ear' and work to decode your patient's message, you are far more likely to have therapy proceed constructively. See you all next week."

WHEN DR. B. and I discussed this case later, we realized that this situation also had demonstrated the phenomenon of the Oedipus complex. Eduardo's father had deserted him at about the age of three, at the height of the boy's oedipal period. Then, his primary attachment to his mother and his hostility against his father (who in this period is experienced and viewed as the successful competitor for Mother's love) are in fierce conflict against the boy's striving for independence from his mother. In this striving, his love for and identification with the father ultimately are the means to resolve the conflict. Yet in Eduardo's case, this difficult process, whose resolution Sigmund Freud considered central to healthy development, was traumatically distorted because his father disappeared and was not available when Eduardo needed him most.

In the oedipal stage, the little boy's attachments, in both their loving and hostile forms, are not only extremely strong, but also extremely volatile, switching easily from mother to father and back. Had Sandy recalled what she knew, and had we thought to lead the discussion in this direction, she might have recognized Eduardo's sudden outburst towards her not only as part of the transference, but specifically as transferring oedipal fixations and problems into therapy. But these issues never came up. A seminar can go in many fruitful paths, and the discussion of oedipal issues was one this seminar never took.

Sandy and Transference, Part Two: One Year Later

ABOUT FIFTEEN months later, Sandy presented another situation to us. As the seminar was beginning, she said, "I want to talk about Eduardo again, although I wonder if I should. He certainly has taught me a lot—but it's been a bitter pill! It may have been profitable for me, but that hardly alleviates the pain of making so many mistakes. Still, I want to learn more, and exposing our mistakes here seems to help most of us gain a lot of insight. So here goes.

"Eduardo has made some remarkable progress. He had been diagnosed as dyslexic, but in the last year he not only has learned to read but has become an avid reader. He is excited and pleased with himself. He used to think of himself as stupid. Not anymore. He is beginning to feel that he really is very smart, which he is."

"Did he just bring up reading?" Renee asked.

"No," Sandy replied. "Actually, for a long time he didn't say anything about reading. Then, during one session that just happened to take place during a storm, the roof of my office creaked. He craned his neck up and stared at the ceiling suspiciously. Then he looked at me and said, 'Is that a ghost?' I said, 'Did it seem like a ghost to you?' He said, 'Yes,' and launched into telling me that he was learning a lot about ghosts. I asked him how he was learning that. He said that at school he was allowed to go to the library for one period and pick out anything that he wanted to read. He was reading all he could about ghosts. So that's how I found out that his reading disability had improved."

"What are ghosts?" Dr. B. asked.

"Frankly, I'm not sure what they are or what to make of Eduardo's interest in them," Sandy replied. "Sometimes I think they're real." She laughed as if she were embarrassed to admit this, and added, "When I'm being more mature, I think ghosts are just our own fears projected out."

"They certainly are that," Dr. B. replied. "But what else are they?"

After a moment Sandy said, "Why don't you tell me what you're thinking, Dr. B.?"

"Aren't ghosts dead people?" Dr. B. replied.

"I hadn't made that connection," Sandy replied. "I was

just so pleased that Eduardo could read now and thought he was giving me a present by telling me."

"That may be true," Dr. B. said. "But if a patient says, 'I spend my free time reading all the books I can get about ghosts,' this ought to start us thinking why of all the possibilities in the library, the child is fascinated by ghosts. When a child talks, for example, about ghosts in the closet or in the attic, he probably means the spirits of dead people. Although we don't know yet what in particular Eduardo means when he refers to ghosts, we assume that intelligent ten-year-olds at least vaguely know that ghosts are dead people who come back to haunt us.

"You know," Dr. B. continued. "The Egyptians built pyramids over their dead pharaohs not just to preserve their bodies or to honor their memory, but also to weigh them down with heavy stones."

A few group members laughed.

"It's true. We continue to put gravestones on the tombs of the dead so they won't crawl out and haunt the living."

"There's only one big problem with that," Sandy replied, her voice full of feeling. "They just won't stay there."

"Yes, but it's a good effort," Dr. B. said.

The strong feeling that had suffused Sandy's reply suggested that she had something personal in mind. I thought it would be worthwhile to share a number of possibilities. "No gravestone can put our personal ghosts to rest," I said, "and we are haunted by what we feel the dead people in our lives would have wanted or expected of us. As a patient said to me, 'Ghosts are more effective than real people. You can't walk away from them.' Because these spirits are so frightening, we have to make the attempt to put them to rest. Who are these ghosts? I think that the most frequent ghosts to haunt us are our dead parents, especially if we have failed to make peace with them when they were alive. And how many of us have completely made peace with our dead parents? If one of Eduardo's parents had died, we could proceed from there, but as we had discussed, Eduardo's parents are both still alive."

Sandy nodded and remained silent.

"Other ghosts that can haunt us are the other dead people we have not come to terms with. They might be people we have loved, hated, or felt ambivalently toward, or people to whom we owed an obligation that we never fulfilled. Perhaps they are people we owed an apology we never delivered, whom we left with an impression we wished we had not, or people with whom we regret never having shared the deep feelings we had about them. But whoever this ghost in Eduardo's past is, as therapists we must think about this sort of question. What does it mean personally to Eduardo? A cliché like 'all children enjoy ghost stories' prevents us from asking fruitful questions. When a boy like Eduardo says, 'I read all the ghost stories I can get my hands on,' his therapist has to first ask herself, 'What do ghosts mean, what do they symbolize in general?' and beyond that, 'What do they mean to this child in particular, at this moment in his life?' "

"I did ask Eduardo what ghosts he was interested in," Sandy said. "He told me that he was interested in the difference between poltergeists and angels. I thought that maybe in this way he was telling me about worrying whether he was a 'bad boy' or 'an angel' in his mother's eyes, because that's how she refers to him. Actually, earlier in this session he had talked about whether he and his actions are acceptable or unacceptable to his mother."

Dr. B. shook his head. "When parents tell their child 'You are a little angel,' it sounds as if they are telling the child how good he is. But in a subtle way they are expressing their ambivalence about the *real* child, who can't be all that good, at least not for very long. Angels dwell in heaven, not on earth. To become an angel a child first has to die."

"Whew, yes," Sandy said, inhaling deeply. "His mother

does teach Sunday school. I am sure that has some relevance. But let me get back to the poltergeists who are said to break things and make messes. Eduardo was very interested in that. Despite his mother's being so neat, he himself likes to break things and make messes. Now the books he likes to read . . ." At that, Sandy stopped herself, as if what she had just said had finally made her realize something. "I guess he *was* reading these books for more reasons than just because kids like ghost stories."

Sandy fell silent and seemed unable or unwilling to go on. Dr. B. and I often noticed that the seminar members made remarks that showed they had good insight into the case, but because they spoke quickly, or did not listen to the exact words they were using, they did not consciously recognize what they already knew. So I repeated the chain of thought Sandy had just voiced and tried to get her to think about it more slowly and carefully. I asked her, "So what exactly are these ghosts and poltergeists?"

"The bad parts of himself?" Sandy asked tentatively, still not quite trusting her own insight.

"Your account showed that unconsciously you already knew that," I said. "As you said, these ghosts and poltergeists are projections of parts of his self."

When Sandy remained thoughtful and silent, Jason spoke. "When Dr. B. spoke about the parents wanting 'an angel,' putting the kid already in heaven, I realized the implications of something Sandy said: Parts of Eduardo are acceptable to his mother, but other parts are unacceptable—perhaps so much so that she wants him to kill them in him. It is as if his mother were saying, 'Parts of you are okay, and I accept them as you. But another side of you is devilish. I reject it entirely and you must rid yourself of it.' The solution is for Eduardo to deny these parts of himself, to project them onto the outside, which may be why he is making them ghosts and poltergeists."

"That fits," Sandy said. "Because Eduardo wants to burp and fart and is confused that his doing so is not regarded as all right. He doesn't understand why doing such things are all right with me, but, like many boys his age, when he does it at home, his mother gets very mad at him and says he burps and farts on purpose. Mind you, if he could burp and fart on purpose, he would, but Eduardo says he doesn't know how.

"Eduardo has spent a lot of time working on being a physical being. Lately his play has changed. Rather than making messes, he now makes believe he is a cook who prepares good food and shares it."

Although Sandy seemed ready to move on to an important issue—that Eduardo seemed to feel he had good food to offer to someone he cared about—Dr. B. and I were not ready to give up on the discussion of ghosts. I said, "Since there don't seem to be dead people in Eduardo's past whom he is conflicted about"—when Sandy nodded in assent, I continued—"perhaps he is interested in ghosts because nobody can stop ghosts from burping and farting and doing other things he wished he could do."

"And they sort of tease people," Sandy added. "He would be tempted to tease if he just knew how."

"That certainly sounds like part of it," I said. "But it still just doesn't seem to explain fully Eduardo's interest in ghosts. Maybe you haven't yet thought this all through, Sandy. Try this approach: What would make you so interested in ghosts? Maybe if you try empathizing that way, you can get closer to the full answer."

"At some level I did do that," Sandy replied. "But what interests me is not that ghosts are dead people, but that they can be either good or bad, and whether Eduardo's ghost is good or bad."

"Well, I have encountered very few good ghosts in my life," Dr. B. said. "Have you?"

"I thought I saw my dead grandmother once and hoped she was a blessing, not a curse," Sandy replied.

With this totally unexpected revelation, Sandy opened up the possibility that her personal experience made it difficult for her to recognize the connection between dead people and ghosts, and why she concentrated instead on whether they were good or bad. It would have been inappropriate at this moment to delve into Sandy's life and her relationship with her grandmother. To remind Sandy of the possible connection between ghosts and dead people, Dr. B. said, "Doesn't it seem unusual that ghosts would fascinate a boy who has no dead people he is concerned about in his life?"

"Yes. Both sets of grand . . ." Sandy began, but she stopped herself, put her hand on her head, and stammered for a moment. "Oh! No, no, no, no, you're so—whoops! There *is* a very strong dead person in Eduardo's life. The family would all like to put it out of their minds, just as I had. But there *was* a death under mysterious circumstances that both parents are very reluctant to discuss. I hardly mentioned this the last time I presented Eduardo's case because the family was so keen to keep the matter a secret that at the time I had been told almost nothing about it. But in the past year they told me a little bit more.

"Somehow, it was tied in to an old, bitter family feud, and it directly affected or closely involved several members of Eduardo's immediate family. The facts are unclear. Someone finally told me that one of Eduardo's relatives is suspected of murdering another. But now everyone has become secretive again. No one will tell me any more. My guess is that the truth is such a terrible and embarrassing story that this proud family refuses to give me a clear picture of what actually happened, though it seems clear that it likely is a murder. All the family's adults know what happened, but despite my efforts, they refuse to let me know more about the secret."

Dr. B. was nodding. "Doesn't that make the importance

of ghosts in Eduardo's life clearer and with it the reason why learning about ghosts was so important for him? What also is clearer is the likely origin of his 'dyslexia.'

"Like many cases where a child's inability to read is diagnosed as due to dyslexia, in Eduardo's case I strongly suspect that emotional factors caused his inability to learn to read," Dr. B. went on. "How might this work? He probably was getting the message at home that he was not free to be inquisitive and learn about what piqued his curiosity. So he feared that by reading he would discover matters about which he was supposed to remain ignorant. He knew that his family kept an important secret, which he was not supposed to know. More significant in his case, it was a mysterious death within the family. Part of his fear might have been that since such a death *had* occurred in his family, maybe if he found out what happened when he wasn't supposed to, he too might somehow die mysteriously. So for self-protection, it was best not to be able to read, since through reading one finds out things one has not known before. Eduardo's dyslexia, as that of so many other children who had been treated for it psychoanalytically, turned out to be a *need not to know.*

"So what happened in his treatment?" Dr. B. looked around the table. His gaze settled on Sandy. "Eduardo slowly discovered that you not only encouraged him to find out things which were important to him, but that to do so was safe. So he began to read. Since his fear of the consequences had caused the 'reading block,'—as it were, the story about the dead relative's ghost—with his new courage, Eduardo not only read ghost stories avidly, but he brought a book of ghost stories to his session, hoping that in his relationship with you he would find out more about the 'ghost' whose mysterious story had been haunting him.

"Forgive me for being so personal. Although Eduardo's avid reading should have alerted you to how important ghosts were for him, I wonder whether your own experience in seeing your grandmother's ghost, and what that meant to you, made it particularly hard for you to decipher Eduardo's involvement with ghosts? If that is the case, this may have been another example of countertransference, of a therapist's personal experience interfering with her correctly handling material a patient brings into therapy."

"You're probably right," Sandy replied, "but it was not just personal experience with ghosts that stood in my way. This family's great secrecy also prevented me from really understanding what exactly had happened and how it might have affected Eduardo. In fact, my feelings about Eduardo and the transference, not just the countertransference, may be why I sometimes have a hard time thinking clearly about details of his life. He's not allowed to know some clear facts about his family, so out of my empathy with him, I forget things too and can seem dumb about him." Sandy pondered for a moment. "Interesting. I hadn't thought of that before. I seem dumb to you like he seemed dumb at school, not being able to read. In past seminars, you've both said that supervision can reenact transference, that we can act toward a supervisor the way a patient acts toward us. I guess this is one example of that. And I still need to understand this death better. For the past eight months, Eduardo has been seeing his father regularly for visitation. But when I meet with the father, he doesn't want to talk about this death, although he clearly knows a great deal about it."

Sandy looked at Dr. B. "I think I've had enough of ghosts. I'll have to deal with that on my own time with my analyst. Could I go on to something else?"

Dr. B. nodded.

"Now I know you'll tell me that I missed the meaning of this one, too, but Eduardo also brought me another book, one about a coal pipeline that carried slurry from Montana to Texas. Now I didn't know anything about these slurries or think they were too important to his emotional life. They are long pipes that carry coal mixed with water . . .''

"I know all about these slurries," said Dr. B.

"Well I didn't," Sandy responded.

"I think you know about them too. I learned about them when I was a coal miner," Dr. B. joked.

"I certainly was never a coal miner," Sandy replied.

"Oh, I think you were," Dr. B. asserted. "I think we all had our coal-miner stage."

Sandy finally laughed, realizing she was being kidded about the anal symbolism of the book. "I should have realized the connection before," she recounted. "Eduardo read me a paragraph from this book and made a slip. He read it again, and then a third time until I finally woke up and talked about it. He said, 'Sh- . . . wouldn't shurry be a funny word?' When I finally asked about the new word, his answer was neither subtle nor hard to decipher. He said, 'Yes, shurry, like in shit.' Then he talked about the slurry pipe looking just like a sewer. 'Is it a sewer?' he asked. I told him it wasn't quite like a sewer, because its job was to carry the coal to where it was needed. It was like the bowels of the earth, the same way his bowels carried away the waste products his body no longer needed.''

Dr. B. replied. "Why is Eduardo so interested in coal slurries?"

"Because he wants his waste products to be all right too."

"Not just all right. To have real value. While slurry pipes may look like sewers, slurry products are very valuable. This story is so important to Eduardo because he craves that his anal productions, be they farts or feces, be valued."

"Eduardo's mother told me that when he was younger, she gave him enemas whenever his bowels did not move exactly on schedule," Sandy said. "I guess this is why he is very concerned about what comes out of him."

"Why did his mother give him enemas?" I asked.

Sandy spoke very quickly. "Well, right after the divorce she felt very stressed, working and taking care of Eduardo. What I think his mother needs to hear is that even though she did the best she could, the enemas were hard for Eduardo."

"Many mothers are divorced or separated, suffer emotional and financial hardships as a result, and unfortunately have to work at jobs that subject them to severe stress and pay ridiculously low wages," I said. "Yet most don't try to solve their problems by giving their sons enemas. So this mother was using enemas for a psychological reason."

"When his mother discusses enemas with me, she gives me the sense that these enemas almost have an erotic connection. Actually, just a few weeks ago, Eduardo mentioned that his mother still bought enema bottles."

"That Eduardo's mother still talks with him about enemas, or at least he knows that she still buys enema bottles for her own use, suggests the mother's continuing emotional involvement in enemas and in elimination," I said. "Those connections keep alive whatever feeling he may have had when his mother gave him enemas in the past. Think about his involvement in farting, his interest in the coal slurry, which traced back, as he put it, to shit."

I spoke directly to Sandy. "Since Eduardo chose to talk to you about the enemas, they still are the source of a complex psychological conflict or have come to symbolize one."

"Don't you think that, like all kids, he is interested in sex, and if that's the way the mother is sexual, he wants to know about it?" Bill said.

"Children are interested in knowing all the secrets of adults, whatever they may be," Dr. B. said. "It is interesting to notice what was kept secret from children in different historical periods. It used to be that finances were an open book and sex was a secret. Now our priorities are turned around. But although we want to be open about sex, we still give what children among themselves call 'useless information.' Because we know how difficult giving sexual information correctly is, we do not talk about sexual *feelings*, which is what the child can understand.

"So let's consider the feelings connected with enemas. On the surface, enemas may be viewed as aggressive, since they violate the child's body, intruding upon it without his permission and usually against his wishes. Enemas force the bowels to give up their contents. Under the best of circumstances, even the child who receives an enema the pediatrician prescribes (which the parents, therefore, consider to be a fundamentally positive experience) not only experiences being overpowered by a parent and having his body forced to give up its contents but also, assuming that the child has been constipated, expels a bowel movement, which probably made the child uncomfortable and provides great and immediate relief.

"So at a minimum, during the enema the child experiences aggressive-intrusive elements merged inextricably with great relief: a confusing, perplexing combination of contradictory feelings. Very often the child resists the enema. To administer it, the parents have to restrain the child, and they may also try to soothe the child to make the enema less traumatic. So here, too, the child experiences aggressive and caring feelings intertwined.

"If, in addition to all the child's complex feelings, his parent has very mixed, or erotic, feelings about elimination—which are by no means rare, since many parents have failed to resolve their own ambivalence about their toilet training—such a welter of feelings is aroused that the child has a very hard time sorting them out. But one memory remains with the child under even the best of circumstances: the fact that his body was rushed to perform as the parents wished rather than at its own pace. Since, as Freud said, the first ego is a body ego, this experience can damage the child's image of himself as a competent individual.

"And in this situation, Eduardo's mother was preoccupied, rushed, and overwhelmed. So it is quite possible that the enemas were the occasions on which she gave her son the most undivided attention he received from her. If this is so, this would have made the enemas even more important to Eduardo because they were the times when he was closest to his mother and had her most exclusively to himself. And what was transpiring excited her. We know that the boy's aim in the oedipal period is to have his mother completely to himself, undivided by her attention to her spouse. Since Eduardo's mother was deeply involved in his elimination during his oedipal period, and his father was gone, that may have eroticized the process further."

"I'm trying very hard to help Eduardo with his feelings about elimination," Sandy said. "If anything, he amazes me so much that I often feel I push him forward too fast. I do trust that he'll work it out, but I find myself just wanting to get in there, make it happen faster, and take more of the credit for it."

"Why not trust that he is going to work it out himself, as he's been doing in therapy with you?" I asked. "By rushing him, aren't you in danger of repeating in the transference relationship his mother's not trusting Eduardo's body to get his stools out?"

"Realizing that is why I presented him today," Sandy said. "During our session two weeks ago, I felt that it was time to make an interpretation, but then I stopped myself, because I suddenly thought that making an interpretation at that time would have been intrusive."

"It is as if you were telling yourself to stop trying to do too much," I said. "Because if you push Eduardo, he will sense that you, the therapist he has confidence in, really distrusts his ability to work it out himself."

Sandy shook her head. "Consciously, distrusting him is exactly the opposite of what I've been trying to achieve. Eduardo is such a terrific kid, but I continually have to resist this temptation to push him. Now that we're discussing it, I realize that it is what I've been struggling with. It's stranger because I would say that this kid has proved to be very good at knowing what he needs and how to work it out."

"From your description I have no doubt that Eduardo is using therapy very well," Dr. B. said. "But in itself, that can be seductive, making a therapist want to do even more and better. Maybe that's what's happening with you and Eduardo."

"So I ought to just let him go at his own pace?"

"Isn't that what your intuition was telling you when you resisted the temptation to make an interpretation?" I said. "Only Eduardo knows how long he has to work on a problem. You can't decide for him."

"And another matter is at stake," Dr. B. said. "The best experience a patient can have during treatment is that he solves his own problems, because that gives him the inner security that he will be able to do so in the future. That is why in psychoanalysis the patient has to take charge of his own treatment. If you solve his problems and seem like a magician to him, when he leaves therapy he leaves subject to your authority. But the analyst's goal is to discharge him with a conviction about his own competence."

"This reminds me that Freud used the image of the analyst as a switchyard," I said. "The analyst can only throw switches that may help shift the direction in which the train is going. But he can't give it power."

Dr. B. nodded. "Which is why if a parent asks you how long it will take until the child is finished with therapy, all you can answer is 'until your child is well.' Even though the therapist's occasional response to what the patient is saying or doing is designed to move the treatment ahead, it ought not to be of a nature that undermines the patient's sense of control over his own treatment.

"Often a patient who is being pushed to move faster will sense that his therapist wishes to be in charge of what is going on. The child who has suffered from the destructive effects of his parents' dominance—as is true for so many children who are psychiatric patients—is not going to be healed by exchanging one domination for another, even the therapist's more benign dominance. Although the therapist knows so much more, the patient will be healed only if he has the experience that he controls his own therapy and life."

"That's what Eduardo is struggling for," Sandy said, "to do things on his timing and with his understanding, rather than constantly adjusting to the people taking care of him. I know I should stay silent more often rather than trying to push him. But somehow I feel guilty about it, as if I'm not doing my job."

"Sitting back and taking the risk that things will take their course is among the hardest things in a therapist's work, maybe even in our own lives," Dr. B. replied. "But why do you feel guilty about remaining silent and letting Eduardo work things out?"

"Because for most of my life *I've* waited for things to take their course," she said. "And now I'm at a point, and am examining this in my own analysis, when I think that in my own past I should have worked harder and made things happen. I feel I do my patients the same disservice if I am too laid-back."

"That's so interesting," Dr. B. said. "Not only is transference at play here, which is essential, but your countertransference also is interfering with your ability to deal comfortably with Eduardo's issue. Many beginning therapists, aware that their expertise is lacking, worry about whether they are conducting therapy as well as they ought to. Out of this anxiety, they push the patient to do better or to progress faster in an attempt to convince themselves that they are doing their job.

"In your situation, Dr. Salauri, thinking that you should have made things move faster in your own life is aggravating the transference phenomenon. Your wish that Eduardo would move faster was motivated both by your desire to cope with your fear that you were not doing your job and by your concern that, in your life, you had let things drag on. Your openness about what motivates you is a pleasure, because it lets us get at these important issues. And your motive is good: You do not want the same to happen in Eduardo's therapy."

Picking up on Sandy's remark that she feared to be "too laid-back," Dr. B. said, "The way you phrase your concern implies passivity, but psychotherapy requires both active and free-floating attention, hardly an attitude of passivity. The psychotherapeutic stance is not a laid-back attitude. In fact, your careful attention to what the patient is saying, more than anything else you can do, convinces the patient of his importance to you and how seriously you take him. When we listen and watch carefully, we convince the patient that his unconscious is very intelligent and revealing. And silence on the therapist's part gives the patient time and space to do things his own way. So, even though we work somewhat differently with children, with Eduardo it would probably be best to trust that he's working it out in his own manner, at his own good pace."

"But how will he get over the damage these enemas did?" Sandy said.

Dr. B. thought over the question and replied. "Probably the best way for Eduardo to overcome them will be for him to separate what was positive and what was negative in them. Then you can help him to become convinced that now he controls his body and with it, by implication, his own life, in the present and future.

"It is *Eduardo* who has to separate the good from the bad in his relationship to his mother, so that he can see how he can get the good feelings in other relationships, without simultaneously accepting the bad ones that his mother foisted on him. And he has to learn to live with parts of himself that are cruel and destructive, to tame them and harness their energy for constructive ends. Only by doing this can he overcome the damaging influence that the bad aspects of his experience have exerted."

Dr. B. looked around the table at the seminar participants. "Isn't that what psychoanalysis is all about? A patient has to analyze out the elements of a very complicated psychological phenomenon. That's why Freud called it 'psycho-analysis.' Only by artificially isolating in therapy the various elements of complex experiences can the patient deal with them. So actually, psychotherapy is a process of first teasing apart and isolating the elements that in reality form a very complex universe, and then dealing with each, one at a time, because only in this way can they be mastered.

"After all, Freud could have called his creation *psychosynthesis*, which would be a much nicer term. But only the patient, in his own good time, can achieve this synthesis after completing the analysis. The therapist has to help the patient analyze out the elements, which permits the patient to master them in isolation and then to create out of these elements a new, different, better, more liveable synthesis.

"In this case, Eduardo's alliance with his therapist will leave him with the realization that benevolent figures who have different attitudes to life do exist, people who accept him as neither an angel or a devil, but as another human being. Then he can elicit their help in building a new life for himself. Eduardo already began to do so when he used the image of the slurry pipe, which is a valuable way to move coal to where it is needed, conveying that he has come to view his digestive apparatus as a valuable part of his body. As Eduardo comes to feel that his body, his first ego, is valuable, he will love himself better and feel more secure."

Returning to the everyday events of therapy, Dr. B. asked Sandy what Eduardo had done in the most recent session.

"During the last session he played with the police car," Sandy said. "He made up a story in which cars went back and forth. Mostly, I was the one who was speeding. Then he took my car to a repair shop and played that he was teaching me how to fix cars."

The time allotted to this session was nearly over; we could not have hoped for a better ending to it. Eduardo, through his play, had given Sandy a hint that she was trying to move too fast. In therapy, the essence is not how fast one can arrive at one's goals, but how well one has spent one's time on fixing one's life. And a central issue in therapy is to accept that the patient is the only one who knows how to fix his own life, and how much time this repair requires. The patient himself becomes aware of what his problems are, where they originated, how he feels about them, and what he needs to do to cope with them. If out of her own anxiety the therapist tries to speed things up, she prevents the patient from exploring his problems in sufficient detail and depth. So the speeding therapist—or, in the symbolic language of play, her car—has to be stopped and made to go more slowly.

Through play with toys, in the symbolic manner in which the unconscious expresses itself best, Eduardo showed his understanding of what psychotherapy is about and taught his therapist about timing. In teaching Sandy how to fix broken cars—and by analogy damaged lives—Eduardo was learning how to do it himself. Had the therapeutic situation not allowed Eduardo to express himself so eloquently through symbolic play, he might never learn to fix his life. As his play in his latest session indicated, Eduardo was well on his way to doing so.

CHAPTER FIVE

Fathers, Sons, and Freud

D R. MICHAEL SIMPSON had trained at Stanford Medical School's child psychiatry training program in the late 1970s. During training, he had impressed us all with his intelligence, skill, and commitment to patients. Even though he now had his own flourishing private practice, Michael wanted further supervision and a forum in which he could discuss cases with other professionals. So he kept attending the seminar after he had finished his formal training.

Most child psychiatrists also have been trained as adult psychiatrists and continue through their careers to see both child and adult patients. In his seminar, Michael decided to present the case of an elderly patient with whom he was beginning to work. For the seminar group, Michael's case raised many resonant issues about the relationship between fathers and sons, the problems of aging, and the fears shared by both the old and the young of being separated from the people they love. For me, this seminar was particularly poignant given the participation of Dr. B., who was then nearing the end of his eighth decade.

"I need some guidance or at least a clearer perspective on a treatment that is meandering with no focus or goal," Michael began. "The patient is unusual for our group; he is a physician, an eighty-year-old orthopedic surgeon."

"Finally you've found a man older than I am, Dr. Simpson," Dr. B. teased. "Is he still practicing?"

"No."

"So why do you call him a physician?"

"Well, that's a good question."

"Thank you, thank you. That's what I'm supposed to ask."

Everyone laughed and Michael relaxed a little. He had attended the seminar long enough so that Dr. B.'s pointed remarks no longer intimidated him. Michael told me that whenever Dr. B. got under his skin, he thought of his appearance, his impish smile and elfish body, as looking 'kind of like a polished acorn wearing wallabies.' That made him laugh inwardly and relax. He now answered Dr. B. with a quip of his own. "Part of that is my bias. I consider a physician a physician until he dies."

"Physicians never die."

"Yes sir, I guess not," Michael said. "But in contrast to old soldiers, this physician hasn't faded away either. He has just panicked. I'm not just trying to be clever. I said that because panic attacks are what this doctor, whom I will call Dr. Svenson, complains of. I could just as well call him Marcus Welby because, despite his panic attacks, his bearing still is very much that of a TV physician. His manner is formal. He is tall and erect, always wears a suit and a tie that, with his swept-back white hair and professional comportment, make him look distinguished. And he *was* a distinguished orthopedic surgeon in the past; he never lost a patient on the operating table.

"Over the past year, Dr. Svenson has been given a pharmacopoeia of medications, including antidepressants and minor tranquilizers. But he has become debilitated. A few weeks ago, during dinner with his wife and son, he had a panic reaction with palpitations. He was convinced he was having not only a heart attack but a stroke as well, and he was rushed to the hospital in an ambulance. The emergency room physician admitted him, and his private internist did a million-dollar workup. Except for some mild diabetes, he turned out to be in remarkably good health. What Dr. Svenson really seems to fear is declining function and the loss of his mental faculties.

"What also contributes to his current state is that his wife has become a little more independent lately."

"Good for the old lady."

"And not so good for him," Michael said. "He says that if he's too nervous to leave the house or to go on some trip his wife wants to take, she just goes out on her own, which he says is difficult for him. He has been coming to therapy once a week and is very interested in reflecting on his past. He grew up in the upper peninsula of Michigan. His parents were Swedish immigrants living in a company town named Ishpeming.

"Dr. Svenson avoids talking about his father, who worked in the iron mines. The only thing Dr. Svenson let slip was that his father believed that life is all hard work and that pleasure equaled sin. His mother worked as charwoman, maid, and cook from early morning till late at night. So his aunt took care of him and his two younger siblings. For some reason, a company doctor took an interest in him and encouraged his education. When Dr. Svenson traces his fears about his wife, he goes back to a time in childhood when he feared being far from his aunt."

"This doctor impresses me," Dr. B. said. "He not only spontaneously remembers significant aspects of his past but also connects his present panic with childhood events. He tells you that his parents devoted little time to him as a boy. He now fears separation from his wife as once he feared separation from his aunt, who was a stand-in for his mother. Not all eighty-year-olds are this reflective." Dr. B. paused and thought for a moment. "Does this physician have children other than the one son?"

"No. And according to him, this one spends almost no time with him."

"Dr. Simpson. This man is eighty years old with a son who has little interest in him. So what can therapy and what can you as a therapist offer him?"

"Well, that is *the* question," Michael answered. "Dr. Svenson wants to talk about his past, so maybe helping him to understand the roots of his symptoms would be very valuable."

"Isn't trying to cure this man at age eighty somewhat unrealistic?"

"Well, I'm not trying to cure him. If you really want to know the truth, I have absolutely no idea what I ought to do. Dr. Svenson's fear and panic have almost incapacitated him. When I talk with him, he repeatedly says he is terrified that his functioning will decline further and that his mental faculties will deteriorate completely. I guess many eighty-year-olds fear losing their physical and mental abilities. But this man is nowhere near that state. Nevertheless, these fears have taken over his life."

I felt we needed a clearer picture of Dr. Svenson's situation. "As you were talking about Dr. Svenson, I found myself trying to imagine how Dr. Svenson spends a typical day. Does he actually just sit at home almost all the time, panicking over his symptoms, except for the rare time when he goes out and is hospitalized to undergo expensive tests?"

"That's a pretty accurate description," Michael said. "He used to be an excellent diagnostician who kept up with the latest advances. For the past few years, Dr. Svenson's anxiety attacks have scared him so badly that now he entirely ignores his own profession. He stays home all day reading books on mental disorders. As he loses touch with orthopedics, he becomes even more terrified that his mind is deteriorating.

"His first internist thought that Dr. Svenson was depressed and prescribed antidepressants. But they did not work because depression was not the accurate diagnosis."

"Let's say it had been. From your description it sounds like Dr. Svenson is somewhat depressed," I said. "Since we all see depressed people in our work, why not take this opportunity to discuss the state of mind of a severely depressed person. It's hopelessness. What really causes depression is the feeling that you're at fault, no good, and nothing you can do will change that. If this were the accurate diagnosis in Dr. Svenson's case, and you were to start out with the premise that he feels this way, what would your goal as a therapist be?"

"Would you try to help him see how he is contributing to his own depression?" Jason asked.

"Wouldn't that make him feel worse?" I replied. "He would become even clearer about what he might have done wrong and would berate himself more."

"Would you try to remove a depressed person's guilt?" Jason said.

"It is not so easy to relieve a depressed patient's guilt feelings," Dr. B. replied. "The patient has to be well into the process of therapy to do so. While the therapist who says to his patient, 'You *ought* to feel guilty,' or 'You *should* feel inferior,' belongs to the world of *New Yorker* cartoons, the therapist who thinks that *he* can 'remove' his patient's guilt belongs in the caste of priests and saviors. Only the patient can free himself of his guilt feelings and the anger he directs at himself for these transgressions. The way for him to do so is to discover their origin and why his unconscious continues to persecute him for some real or imaginary act, so bad that he thinks he deserves to be punished for it forever.

"Depression distorts the sense of time. If we knew the future, many of us would commit suicide today, because if at this moment we saw the accumulation of all the painful things that will happen to us in our lives, and all the mistakes we will make, we couldn't bear it. But in real life we meet these one by one. That is bearable. How does that differ from the suicidal person? The suicidal individual sees all the painful things that have happened and will happen in his life accumulated together as a single mass. He doesn't realize that he will never encounter them in their accumulation, so he is hopeless and desperate.

"But to answer your question, Dr. Winn," Dr. B. said to Jason, "therapy must restore trust and hope to the patient. Why? Because before a patient can embark on the difficult and painful task of understanding the origin of his guilt feelings, which likely is both in the superego and the id, he must have the courage and strength to do so. We need to help convince him that he can do a lot on the positive side, so he will be able to explore the psychological hell he lives in. And let's not forget that we all survive on trust and hope, not on fact. There's no protection in this world, for example, against people walking out on you, like Dr. Svenson's mother or maybe even his wife. But to be able to function well, we need to hope and believe that it won't happen to us."

I felt we had digressed. "Let's get back to Dr. Svenson," I said.

Michael continued. "As I said, when the antidepressants didn't work, Dr. Svenson went to a psychopharmacologist who stopped them and put him on Xanax, which as you know, is a minor tranquilizer with some antidepressant activity that is particularly useful in treating panic attacks. But that didn't help either. After Dr. Svenson panicked at the restaurant and had been worked up at the hospital, the consulting psychiatrist sent Dr. Svenson to me, and I diagnosed him as suffering from agoraphobia."

"What do you mean by that?" Dr. B. challenged Michael.

"By what?"

"By that word *agoraphobia?*"

Dr. B. often said that language was the psychoanalyst's primary tool; to use it properly required a dictionary. Fascinated by nuance, etymology, and how much these can reveal about the subconscious reasons for a person's choice of words, Dr. B. preferred to use the *Oxford English Dictionary* in its too-large-to-be-lugged form. "In psychoanalysis using the right word—what the French call *le mot juste*—is essential. An approximation won't do. What does that word *agoraphobia* really mean?"

"It's a fear of open spaces, a fear of what's out there that prevents someone from going out," Michael answered.

"You are at a loss about what you can do for this man, Dr. Simpson. What you do will depend on how you diagnose his condition. Which is why I must focus on whether agoraphobia is an accurate diagnosis of what Dr. Svenson suffers from? Are his symptoms really a fear of what's out there? You can call anything by any name. A rose is a rose is a rose. You can call your dachshund a Great Dane. He won't object; only it doesn't make him a Great Dane."

I interposed a question. "Tell us why you think that Dr. Svenson's ailment is best diagnosed as agoraphobia?"

"He dreads being in any situation from which he might not be able to escape," Michael said. "This prevents him from going places. As you know, we all now follow the American Psychiatric Association's manual on diagnosis, DSM III. And Dr. Svenson's symptoms fit DSM III diagnostic criteria for agoraphobia pretty well."

"From a technical standpoint and according to DSM III criteria, you are absolutely right to call him agoraphobic," I said. "The trouble is that by standardizing diagnosis DSM III tends to draw the therapist away from the unique individual he is treating. Using this technical term dissuades you, his therapist, from asking yourself what his symptoms mean to him. What does it mean that Dr. Svenson fears he is losing his mind and that he seems terrified of going out?

"Even those observations and symptoms are general. As his therapist, you want to know what specific feelings or experiences unique to Dr. Svenson underlie his fears. What brought on his panic at *that* meal? I think it is very likely that it was some psychological trigger. The 'million-dollar workup' must have ruled out a stroke, dementia, and other indubitably organic diseases that cause terrible panic states, such as pheochromocytoma. Perhaps the internists missed some possible organic cause, but given the quality of the medical workup, that seems unlikely. So to comprehend the symptom and, more importantly, what Dr. Svenson might be trying to achieve or say unconsciously through having it, you need to discover what that trigger was and what it meant."

I continued the thought. "This brings up a more general issue we all face as therapists. Physicians know that human illnesses have many causes. But the body can express illness in only a limited number of final common pathways. Treatment based only on symptoms can be very harmful. For example, although all pneumonias present more or less only one general set of pulmonary symptoms, such as a cough, many different microorganisms and chemical irritants can cause pneumonia. To treat it correctly, we first must know which cause our treatment has to attack. If we simply treated the patient's cough with codeine to suppress it, we would make the person feel slightly better temporarily, but we could do great harm to the patient in the long run. Without the cough, the patient doesn't clear his lungs, and this could make an infection worse, and the underlying illness would progress unchecked. Good medical care means figuring out why the person is coughing and treating the cause and, if possible, curing the individual.

"In a similar fashion, agoraphobia is a symptom; people become agoraphobic for different reasons or use it defensively to achieve different purposes. Perhaps there is even a biological predisposition to it. But if there is, not everyone with this tendency becomes ill or agoraphobic in the same way. For instance, some people are agoraphobic because they fear the outdoors. Others need at all times to remain close to some person for a particular reason. Unconsciously, Dr. Svenson's agoraphobia is designed to get him something. But it fails to do so. If his anxiety really were about going out, he probably would not have gone to that restaurant of his own free will. So something else other than just going out must have triggered that panic attack in the restaurant. We ought to try to understand the particular reasons Dr. Svenson has for becoming agoraphobic, Michael. Then you will be in a better position to help him diminish his anxiety through psychotherapy."

Dr. B. took off his glasses, leaned back in the chair, and thought for a while. Then he put his glasses back on and spoke. "The fact that his particular panic attack happened at a restaurant might be very significant. On the other hand, the trigger might have been something incidental, something that just happened to occur there by chance and made Dr. Svenson panic. It is best not to jump to premature conclusions. However, you can expand your thinking if you speculate about what it may have been that brought about a feeling in Dr. Svenson so intense that he thought he was dying.

"From what you have told us, his mother had a very difficult life. She worked hard and probably had very little time left over for him. And now you say that his wife is leaving him alone more often. One possibility is that his 'agoraphobia' is related to his wife's absences, based on his ancient fear about being far from his aunt. But the symptom also is trying to achieve a purpose. It may represent his attempt to undo the tragedy of his childhood: his mother's absence and his rage at being separated from the woman he needed so desperately.

"In a more speculative vein, since in the most primitive sense mothers are connected with feeding, Dr. Svenson's anxiety might have become accentuated while he was eating in a restaurant, in a social eating situation, because feeding symbolizes his tie to his mother. To the child, nurturing is an act of affection. Therefore, in the deepest sense, the ability to love has much more to do with how the child was fed and nursed. If the nursing or nurturing experience was right, positive, or whatever, we want to re-create it all our lives. So in this speculative vein, Dr. Svenson's symptoms might have represented a symbolic effort to have his mother stay at home to care for him.

"Or perhaps the fact that Dr. Svenson's son was at this meal was more central to why Dr. Svenson panicked there. After all, you mentioned that he had a difficult relationship with his father and perhaps has not had a good one with his son."

Dr. B. spoke softly to Michael. "These ideas, and any others we may discuss, must be regarded simply as working hypotheses that further therapeutic exploration will confirm or disprove. We must avoid getting too attached to any one speculative line of thinking about such matters, because then we have too hard a time of giving it up. That's true for every scholarly and scientific endeavor. It is hard not to get attached to some particularly elegant hypothesis in science. But that can make it hard to see that, elegant though the hypothesis is, it is not true.

"I do not know what triggered Dr. Svenson's panic at that particular time and place. But it was not generalized agoraphobia. It was something specific."

"Do you object to all generalizations in psychotherapy?" Michael asked.

"Would you like being treated as a representative of a large group, especially by your psychotherapist?" asked Dr. B. "We all want to be considered individuals. Generalizations are seductive, but every person and situation is unique. If the therapist is satisfied with generalizations where his patient is concerned, he usually will deprive the patient and mislead himself. Because what is interesting to Dr. Svenson, and ultimately to us as psychotherapists, is not how he resembles a group of patients, but what is unique about him.

"In an effort to become more 'scientific,' many psychotherapists draw on studies that report generalizations about patients and their behavior. In academic psychology or sociology, these generalizations perhaps have to be based on looking at external characteristics you can see and, better yet, count. Yet no one has really come up with a good way to quantify the enormous variety of inner life. In trying to use the scientific methods, the researcher looks for patterns and generalizations, ignoring the specific and unique. When two people give similar replies to a question, researchers tend to be satisfied with putting these similar replies into one box. By doing that, these two people are in one measurable category. Most researchers do not try to examine the difference in replies, or try to discern whether different motives or purposes may lie behind the similar replies.

"For example, a lot of research has been done on the age at which teenagers become sexually active. When a person tells the researcher when they had their first sexual experience, what is communicated is a date or an age. Few of these studies are interested in the individual's subjective response or what the sexual experience *meant* to him or her. In these studies it does not matter whether the teenager enjoyed their first experience or found it so disgusting that they abstained from sexual activity for years afterwards. So what does this statistic mean: 'age of first sexual activity'?"

Dr. B. went on. "This is why most academic psychological

and sociological research is so different from the psychotherapy, based on psychoanalytic insights, that interests us
in this seminar. Only clinical teaching, based on individual
cases, teaches how important the specific is. In clinical work,
a generalization makes sense only when it is firmly anchored
in its concrete origins."

"But Freud made generalizations," Michael said.

"Yes, he did," Dr. B. replied. "But generalizations were
not how he invented psychoanalysis. This discipline did not
come about because certain abstract ideas about the unconscious sprang into Freud's head from out of nowhere. He
invented psychoanalysis because he said, 'I've seen these patients who behave in a way I don't understand.' Then he said,
'These are the dreams of one person I know very well—me.
Where have they come from? What do they mean? What do
they say about me, a unique person with unique experiences
to which I react in unique ways?' Only after he clarified all
these specifics did he try to arrive at a theory about dream
interpretation.

"But your point is valid, Dr. Simpson. Perhaps we still suffer in some ways from the fact that Freud tried to generalize
too quickly. After all, he wanted to convince the public about
the validity of his findings. And in talking to the public, I think
he did so with an overreadiness to arrive at generalizations."

"Back home we'd call him a young man in a hurry." Michael smiled and continued with his case description. "Dr.
Svenson often is afraid to leave his house. As soon as he tries
to step outside, he feels light-headed, as if the room were
spinning. His perceptions become distorted: People and objects actually seem to be moving away from him. These reactions do sound like agoraphobia to me, so I was planning
to intervene with some standard agoraphobia treatment. I
know you don't like that treatment, but I have found it helpful
in other cases."

Dr. B. started to speak, but Michael went on. "I planned gradually to get him comfortable with the situations he was avoiding, using a desensitizing behavior therapy, and . . ."

"Wait," Dr. B. interrupted. Michael looked surprised; Dr. B. spoke on. "You're going too fast for me. Let's examine what you are telling us. Weren't you saying something about this symptom's symbolic meaning? Doesn't this 'panic,' brought about by people and objects seeming to move away, sound like anxiety about losing contact and touch—in fact, like separation anxiety?"

Dr. B. paused and looked around at the group. "I can see that you all have reactions to my interrupting Dr. Simpson just now, and I want to explain to you why I did so and have done so on other occasions. It was not because I wanted to belittle anything he was saying—far from it. But I was afraid that if he went on with that train of thought, we all would lose sight of something extremely important.

"As a teacher, I am obligated to listen to Dr. Simpson carefully. That is what I owe to you all." He glanced at Michael. "If I had let you go on, I might have lost an insight my unconscious had just produced from feeling a sympathy with Dr. Svenson, which easily could have eluded me."

Dr. B. looked around the table. "Many of you press us to explain points in a technical way. Usually we resist. But in this case, a technical explanation might be helpful. Conscious attention is an orderly ego function, which is inimical to that which emerges only tentatively, fleetingly, from the unconscious. So I had to get hold of this evanescent insight before it escaped me." Dr. B. looked at Michael again. "The only way I knew how to do this was to prevent myself from listening to what you were saying about desensitizing behavior therapy, to which, as you know, I have a strong negative reaction. If I kept focusing on your words, my strong feelings might have tempted me to respond to what you might say about this method of therapy instead of concentrating on a fleeting insight I had about Dr. Svenson.

"What suddenly struck me emerged from your reporting that, in his panic, Dr. Svenson sees people and objects moving away from him. I suddenly realized that the source of his panic might not be the fact that he was 'outside' the house in an open space, but it might have emerged from this 'moving away' sensation. From what you have told us, I wonder whether this old man, so near the end of his life, can be any different from the rest of us? What, after all, is death like? Don't we consider it the ultimate separation from all that we love?

"Old people ponder the end and fear they will lose contact with what they love—that it all will 'move away' from them forever. Anxiety about losing our mother and later about losing a wife or someone else who we love deeply is the only guideline we have to understanding this anxiety about the ultimate loss. Separation anxiety thus serves as a forerunner of death anxiety.

"Infantile experiences are so important because all other experiences stand under the shadow of the first one. So the panic a crying infant feels, the utter anguish at being alone and uncomforted, may be the template on which we build our image and give form to our dread of death. Now how can a man Dr. Svenson's age hope to counteract this powerful anxiety?"

"That's exactly what I am here to find out," Michael replied, sounding almost relieved.

"I'll tell you how," Dr. B. went on. "Only through feeling that he leaves something of himself behind or someone connected to him who will continue, who will not 'move away.' "

Michael smiled, his voice was animated. "And Dr. Svenson may be finding that continuity hard to establish because he has little to do with, in fact is even somewhat hostile toward, his son."

"Isn't that sad?" Dr. B.'s tone softened. "From what you said, I suspected that if this doctor had a good, ongoing relationship with a son, he would not need psychotherapy. I wasn't sure, but I suspected it might be the case, because, after all, his son was also at the meal where Dr. Svenson became so anxious. That led me to suspect that Dr. Svenson is so disappointed in his son, or his wife, or both, that he felt as if he were dying.

"What he needs now is a positive relationship with a young man. You are a young physician yourself, beginning to make a professional life for yourself and to build your practice. That might make you a very suitable subject of interest for this old doctor."

"But if I become his friend, won't I jeopardize my role as his therapist?" asked Michael.

"I'm not suggesting that you abandon your job as his psychiatrist. But from that position, you can show a supportive interest in Dr. Svenson, his life and his achievements. That a bright, sophisticated young physician like you is interested in what Dr. Svenson has accomplished, and finds his achievements admirable, would be most encouraging to him.

"In fact, doing so is one of the best things you can do for an old patient. Showing that interest will give him a positive image of his achievements. By encouraging Dr. Svenson to talk about them to you, an appreciative listener, you will help him achieve something more. You will help him bring his accomplishments to life again. If all goes well, this could help him see his life not only as having been meaningful in the past but also as having meaning to someone of importance in the present—his psychiatrist.

"In contrast," Dr. B. went on, "even if with your help Dr. Svenson came to understand in great detail what childhood events had contributed to his pathology, the insight would not help him integrate his personality in a new, better way. What motivates us as therapists in most situations is the hope that through our work together, the patient can build a new life for himself, which he will be able to live for many years. But unfortunately, no therapist can do this for Dr. Svenson. His life is practically over, give or take a few years. After fifty, with rare exceptions, and certainly after sixty, building a new life for the future just doesn't make sense any more. But if this distinguished physician had a positive perspective on his past life, he would have the strength to weather whatever emotional problems he has in the present."

Michael sounded puzzled. "Why can't a person renew himself at fifty or sixty?"

"Just try to!" Dr. B. said. "More power to you if you can. But remember that not so long ago, life expectancy was thirty or forty. With age, the machine just runs down, the energy wanes, and things you once found simple take far more concentration and effort."

"I think you have something there," Michael said thoughtfully. "At our last session, Dr. Svenson asked to see me more often, and then he said: 'Don't expect any metamorphosis from me, but I would like to feel more positive about some relationships I have now.' "

Dr. B. looked pleased. "When you gave your initial description didn't I say that Dr. Svenson struck me as an intelligent, reflective man? You know, psychotherapy with older people is not discussed often enough. I think this is because Freud spent his life treating patients who were at most in early middle age, trying to help them achieve more meaningful, well-lived lives. In his long life, Freud contended with illness, infirmity, and old age, but wrote little about treating elderly patients. He focused his attention on his struggle to overcome his oedipal inhibitions, but told us little about his emotional life as an elderly father.

"Like Freud, many psychotherapists prefer working with younger patients who have their lives ahead of them. Others have personal aversions to treating the elderly." Dr. B. nodded towards Michael. "Fortunately for Dr. Svenson, I don't sense that you feel that way. But a therapist has to handle some matters differently when working with someone old. As Dr. Svenson told you, at his age even a man of great achievements does not realistically expect to make enormous changes in his way of life. He knows that at his age, you don't try to rebuild the house you live in; by age sixty it's built. But you still can become more comfortable living in it. Dr. Svenson still can have some very interesting and rewarding years left, and learn to live in more satisfying ways than he is presently doing. That will make his life better.

"Freud gave us an excellent example of how one man used his profession to contend not only with old age but also with the ravages chronic illness inflicted on him, something Dr. Svenson has been spared. For Freud's last sixteen years, he had cancer of the jaw. He underwent over twenty operations, used a wooden dental prosthesis, and lived in terrible discomfort. But he had a passion that made life worth living: Discovering more about people, expanding his theories and insight, and passing ideas on to the next generation were so important to him that they gave him energy to carry on. He wanted to make certain that the discipline he had devoted so much of his life to creating would continue after he died.

"I would even speculate that when Freud wrote, his pains did not bother him as much as at other times. Despite old age, illness, and suffering, his functioning as an author and scholar was excellent. His work was important to others and to the progress of this new discipline. That, and what he saw as his mission in life, kept him going. His example is a good model for the rest of us."

"How does that apply to Dr. Svenson?" Michael said.

"Let's start with what he is trying to tell you when he says that he wants to see you more often. I think he is telling you that taking tranquilizers and other drugs has done him no good. Talking once a week about his successes and achievements in the past is not enough to make his present anxieties disappear. But it is going in the right direction. Dr. Svenson knows he has to do more work in psychotherapy, and that is why he wants to see his psychiatrist more often.

"If I wanted to be fancy, I could add that he is also saying, 'Since you have shown respect for me, you will show respect for my anxieties.' Now what does 'respect for his anxieties' mean in a person who says that he is not going to remodel his whole personality?"

A few silent moments passed, and no one seemed to have a clear idea. Then Michael offered, "To accept that his anxiety is there for a good reason?"

"That's right," Dr. B. said. "This respect for anxieties is exactly the difference between insight-oriented work and the behavior therapy you mentioned before. Behavior therapy promises to free you of your symptom *regardless* of what caused it—with not much consideration to the important functions the symptom might serve, or what the person is trying to achieve and communicate through it."

"Could you elaborate on that idea," Gina said. "I want to be sure I am following."

When Dr. B. did not answer right away, I picked up the discussion. "Respecting a symptom means trying very seriously to understand its causes and its importance in the person's whole makeup, assuming that this symptom is not an alien body to be cut out and thrown away as useless. In this way, the therapist conveys his appreciation for the person's intelligence and gives the patient a message: 'I respect your attempt to try to solve your problem through a symptom. Don't call yourself crazy or idiotic for having it. Hopefully, in our work together, we will figure out what you were trying to achieve and say through the symptom, what important feeling you might have been trying to preserve or hide from. Then, you may decide to devise a less detrimental way to accept your feelings, reach your goals, or communicate your message.'

"Often, in treating children, who are not as able to express themselves verbally, the therapist is prone to treat the child and his symptom as just something to be gotten rid of, particularly when the therapist finds the symptom obnoxious. But in my experience, what the child makes of this is that the therapist considers himself a representative of a 'superior' civilization who wants to teach this 'idiot' or 'savage' good behavior. Naturally, the child resents this attitude and feels provoked to act out against the person who is insulting him."

Dr. B. paused, took off his glasses, and lay them on the table's polished top. After a few moments of silence, he put his glasses back on and then spoke in a quiet voice directly to Michael. "You clearly respect Dr. Svenson intrinsically. Perhaps as a physician yourself, you even identify with him as a distinguished colleague. Despite the behavior therapy you mentioned, you have been respecting Dr. Svenson's symptoms. But I wonder whether you went too fast because you were led into therapeutic overoptimism or haste, which is dangerous for both patient and therapist."

"But this man is open psychologically. I don't want to leave him at his present level," Michael protested.

"I never suggested that you do," Dr. B. replied. "After all, what this formerly successful and productive physician is doing now is not very constructive."

When Dr. B. spoke again, his voice was soft and reflective. "I don't think one has to meet death with courage. But I think that this intelligent, previously professional man could do more with his remaining time than swallow a wide variety of pills or contemplate falling into insanity."

"Some older people manage to go on just because they get a helpful variety of pills that stops them from falling into insanity," Michael said.

"But that's not the case with this man," replied Dr. B. "Dr. Simpson, you can do something very important by showing him that. It sounds like he desperately needs someone, and perhaps something, in which he takes an interest, something that will rekindle his interest in life. Far from being a hopeless case or a man near death, Dr. Svenson sounds quite sturdy and probably would be far sturdier if he didn't take all those antidepressant pills and if he felt that what he did with his time was useful. Every old man needs to know that his life still has some value to somebody—not in the past, but now, in the present.

"Obviously, if Dr. Svenson has a bad relationship with his son, this son will not be too interested in building him up. Dr. Svenson needs someone like a son to build him up, and so, in a way, that is the role I am suggesting for you. At the same time, you must realize that this is very difficult psychological work because, as a therapist, you cannot permit yourself to act out.

"For example, you must not pretend, or in your own mind proceed, as if you actually were Dr. Svenson's son. You also must resist the temptation to behave as if he were your own father. In other words, you must not step out of your role as his concerned psychotherapist. You must not directly suggest to Dr. Svenson what he should or should not do with himself.

"This is another of the great pitfalls of psychoanalytic psychotherapy: The therapist often is tempted to try to arrange the external aspects of a patient's life, essentially making decisions for the patient. Even though such suggestions might be well meant and pertinent, this always is detrimental because it weakens the patient.

"So even while the therapist might have such suggestions in mind, he ought to refrain from stating them directly. Instead, he must gradually lead patients to make their own decisions and gain strength from the fact that they can take major aspects of their lives into their own hands."

"And the therapist must be ready to have the patient make a decision that is very different from the one the therapist had in mind," I said.

Dr. B. went on. "The reason such direct suggestions harm patients is the patient can never be sure whether the decision was his own or if he was manipulated. Being manipulated weakens the patient's ego, while the conviction that he arrived at a decision about his life on his own strengthens it. In Dr. Svenson's case, the therapist is actually of an age where he could be Dr. Svenson's son or even grandson, and thus the temptation to give advice is very strong. However, many other dangers are inherent in Dr. Simpson's giving this patient direct advice. Just one of the many is that the therapist could unconsciously be acting out a remnant of his own oedipal conflict."

Dr. B. glanced at Michael. "While you have given us no reason to think you have been so tempted, you have to be careful to avoid this possibility. So what should you do to tread this fine line? Let's say that Dr. Svenson complains that he feels light-headed, that he experiences people and objects moving away from him, and that these symptoms stop him from teaching orthopedic surgery residents. You might concentrate not on these significant symptoms, but instead you might reflect on what a remarkable and enviable record Dr. Svenson had as a surgeon who never lost a patient. He must have been extraordinarily skillful and in tune with the needs of his patients to have achieved that. You could emphasize that Dr. Svenson's skill is unusual and should be taught to others, something he did while he was practicing. Now maybe Dr. Svenson won't consider teaching again, but your appreciating him, and your conviction that Dr. Svenson still has something unique to teach and give *now*, would be therapeutic all by itself."

"My guess is that Dr. Svenson keeps coming to you because he is fed up with doctors who feed him pills. You can let him know that you are interested in helping him find a workable solution, not in prescribing palliatives that, at best, give him only symptomatic relief. This might give him the courage to believe with you that a positive solution is possible."

Michael seemed taken aback. "I'm confused. Are you saying that even though you don't believe a cure is really possible, I should lie and not convey that to Dr. Svenson?"

"I think that a cure of his anxiety attacks is possible," Dr. B. said. "Also, I am certain that if he became active again, his anxiety would recede.

"I am not suggesting that you give him false hope or lie. Not by any means. It's not so much that I'm against it on moral grounds, although a good case can be made for that. I could never lie because I feared that I would be found out, and the lie would then serve no purpose or would be destructive. It is too difficult to remember what lie one has told to whom, and then the lie is apt to be recognized as that. But even more importantly, lying would be a continuous impediment to my spontaneity. We're all more at ease if we tell the truth. And a man as intelligent as Dr. Svenson is would sense that you are lying and would lose all trust in you.

"What I was saying is not possible for Dr. Svenson is the restructuring of his personality, which usually is the goal of psychoanalytic psychotherapy. He told you that himself. He comes from a poor, hard-working family. His climb was difficult; he probably achieved what he did at great expense to himself. When such an intelligent, reflective man does not want to talk much about his father, one has to assume from the little he did say that his relationship with his father was not a good one, which may be part of why his relationship with his son is not good."

At this point, Bill asked, "How do you make the jump from the bad relationship with his father to the bad relationship with his son?"

"Bill," I said, "this is one good example of the *repetition compulsion*. We usually use the term to mean that we repeat our childhood conflicts over and over. But in another sense, the term also implies that in strange ways people repeat the lives of their parents, with certain modifications. Unfortunately, usually it is the problematic areas that are repeated, precisely because they involve unresolved conflicts. So, like moths to a flame, many people, and all of us on some occasions, seem to instinctively seek out what will damage them, or repeatedly induce the re-creation of relationships that have wounded them deeply. A person whose parent has hurt him terribly swears that he will be different when he has children. Yet often, years later he has, in fact, reenacted his relationship to his parent in his relationship to his child, exactly what he swore he would never do.

"It's hard to entirely avoid doing that. We all do it to some degree. In growing up, everyone develops a basic identification with and a deep attachment to both parents, regardless of whether the parents have been desirable when we view them objectively. Even in relatively good and loving family relationships, we still resemble our parents in our—and their—undesirable traits, but we seldom recognize this. We realize it most clearly when we yell at our children, catch ourselves, and say ruefully, 'I can't believe I said that! I sounded just like my father, and I hated it.' When the parent-child relationship has been bad, the grown-up child often re-creates this relationship with his or her own child, and thus the unhappiness continues anew. For many people, it takes a great deal of psychotherapy to interrupt the cycle."

Bill spoke again. "It must be frightening for Dr. Svenson to realize that so much suffering in his life may have been motivated by forces beyond his control and awareness."

"Isn't that true for everybody?" I said. "Some people enter this field because, without being aware of it consciously, they hope to heal a disturbed parent who was very hurtful, maybe

even destructive. However, simply knowing psychiatric theory won't help very much. Even a person with a library of
intellectual knowledge is motivated by hidden forces. In a
sense, that is the root of human tragedy. It was Oedipus'
ignorance to the true facts about his past that led him inex-
orably to a terrible outcome. Oedipus was a man who prized
knowledge and made a name for himself through solving a
riddle. Yet he did not truly know himself, which led to his
downfall."

"But let's get back to Dr. Svenson," Dr. B. said. "I would
like to know why this man retired at age seventy. That he
retired from an active surgical practice at seventy shows good
sense and a moral concern for his patients, but you can stop
doing surgery yourself and still be a very effective physician.
I know physicians his age who donate their services as they
continue to teach and consult on a part-time basis."

I turned to Dr. B. "You're almost Dr. Svenson's age. If this
man came to you, how would you treat him?"

"I would encourage him to join me in studying him, as a
common venture, engaged in as equals," Dr. B. answered
immediately. "That is, I would arouse his interest in thinking
about his problem with me more or less as a colleague. With
old people—as with children—you have to use yourself much
more. But you can use yourself only in terms of your personal
assets. I am an old man and certainly would reflect back on
past cases, because I have such a lot of experience. Dr. Simpson's assets are those of a young psychiatrist working on his
future, while treating an old surgeon who at his age was very
successfully building his career."

"If you were seeing Dr. Svenson, would you talk about
what it's like to get old, sharing what it's like for you?"
Michael asked.

"Unfortunately, old men are all too keenly aware of what
getting old is like. So I would avoid that subject," Dr. B.

replied. "But since you are not yet at his age, let me tell you a bit about the problems of getting old.

"In old age, everybody fears he will not be able to function as he once did or that Alzheimer's disease or strokes will steal his mind. What the therapist must do is separate the more or less normal reactions to old age from those that are severely pathological exaggerations. Not all unresolved problems are neurotic. Neurosis is spending time on problems not worth spending time on. Mental health is selecting those problems that are important enough to solve. Not everybody responds to becoming old in the same way. But to call it a 'golden age' is a euphemism that covers up the facts. For most people it is the opposite—an age of decline and anxiety about further deterioration.

"The elderly individual frequently experiences deficiencies in health and, in general, feels enfeebled, often no longer able to do things one did with ease when one was younger. So some of Dr. Svenson's worries are natural, given his age. However, by not being able to go out and by expressing an exaggerated fear of losing his mind, he shows them in a pathological way.

"While Dr. Svenson still has his wife, old people usually are acutely aware that their spouse is vulnerable to illness and might die. Part of the fear of old age, particularly when an elderly man or woman loses a spouse, is a fear of loneliness. Actually, Dr. Svenson has no realistic reason to feel lonely, since he still lives with his wife, and she is healthy and sounds lively and eager to take pleasure from the time she has left. Although she has to some degree declared her independence from him, this really resulted from his depression and fear of leaving home, and not because he could not continue to be a good husband.

"In my opinion, it makes a great deal of difference if the husband and wife still live together or if one has died. In general, if one can generalize about such things, women find it less hard to live alone than men do. Part of your task will be to get Dr. Svenson to a point where his marriage improves. If he becomes active again in his field, I'm sure that his marriage and life will get better. In fact, Dr. Svenson is in a much better position than many elderly people. He has a profession in which he can continue being useful if you, his therapist, can help him to become active again. Further, he may then be a little better protected if his wife dies before him, since he still will have some activity that interests him.

"That is why, if I were treating Dr. Svenson, I would focus on his achievements. Imagine what it must have been like to come from a mining town, to work hard and to get through college, medical school, and residency, and then to build a distinguished career. That is a life worth being proud of, whatever his failings as a father may have been. I would talk with him about his tremendous achievements, about his continuous efforts to excel, and about what a high price being so good must have exacted."

"I also would wonder how Dr. Svenson dealt with having had to pay this price," I added. "Some part of his current anxiety might very well be an extension of the anxiety he likely felt in medical school when he worried about whether he was going to make it or whether he would fail and end up back in the mines. That anxiety can persist for a lifetime and make a person feel driven to excel, as if no matter how well they do, they remain always vulnerable to having the life they have created collapse. While we seek emotional security, it remains true that many people actually are spurred to great achievement in an effort to escape insecurity. So if I were seeing him, I might even wonder with him whether some remnant of his anxiety reflects his old resentment at having had to pay so high a price throughout his life, to sacrifice continually for his great achievement. This feeling may still exist, a resentment that, although no longer actual, may remain in his unconscious and may contribute to his anger and fuel his mental paralysis.

"But as Dr. B. has said, your major therapeutic effort needs to be directed to exploring why Dr. Svenson no longer is active, emphasizing what a great shame it is that he abdicated so prematurely.

"This doctor has withdrawn from life and buried himself in books about mental illness," I went on. "Many old people withdraw into themselves because for them the world has become an awful, anxiety-arousing place. So, Michael, if you tell Dr. Svenson that the world has a great deal to offer him, he is so immersed in his anxieties that you could easily sound Pollyannaish to him. He might even think, 'This kid just doesn't understand what life is really like.' So in the end, Dr. Svenson would only doubt your intelligence and maturity.

"But if you said, 'A man like you could remain active, useful, and admired by people, something we all like and enjoy. What stops you from doing that?' You're not talking about the world but about Dr. Svenson as an individual and what he might offer. You're implying that you have hope that Dr. Svenson can improve his situation and that you believe that Dr. Svenson has a great deal to offer young physicians. Helping Dr. Svenson focus on that important issue just might draw him out of his ruminations and toward mental health. And Dr. Svenson might even accept that you, this young physician who is his therapist, might be more knowledgeable than he is about what kind of teacher young physicians appreciate.

"What is so pathological in Dr. Svenson's present mental state is that he is not using his assets to prove his value to himself and to encourage himself when he feels useless, fearful and paralyzed. What we have to try to understand is why he avoids a positive solution to his problem that seems obvious to others."

"I'm not sure I follow," Michael said.

"This doctor feels hopeless about himself," Dr. B. said. "Therefore, we have to restore hope to him. We cannot restore hope for a new love relationship or for another fifty years of successful life. We can only restore hope that he can still do something interesting and worthwhile with the time he has left. And one way for him to start down this path is for a person who could be his son, an up-and-coming physician he might even wish his son resembled, to have trust in him and to think that Dr. Svenson is a good, worthwhile individual. You must feel confident that you can restore this hope to him, that, even though he is quite old, Dr. Svenson still can get some pleasure from life.

"To restore hope, you must believe that the psychotherapy you practice gives you the ability to do so. If you are not convinced that to some degree, however small, you can be of help to the patient, you should leave the person to their own devices or refer them to someone else. But with a patient you have felt you could help, the worst mistake you can make is to start feeling defeated yourself about what you can do for him or, for that matter, any other patient you believe can improve. A patient can get you worried. A patient can keep you up all night thinking about him. A patient can get you to the library to read for hours trying to figure out how to understand and help him. But you must never let a patient defeat you. Not because you have some machismo need to win, but because defeatism in the psychotherapist is the most destructive thing that can happen to a patient. If the therapist feels defeated, the patient can not develop hope for himself.

"Let's remember that, in general, anybody who goes into therapy feels defeated by the very fact that he has to enter treatment. Entering psychotherapy is a blow to one's self-esteem that makes one feel inferior. Internists and surgeons deal with that all the time with their physically ill patients. The good bedside doctor will try to assure the patient that no matter how sick he is, there is hope for him. The physician points out how much of the patient's body still functions normally and how many powerful interventions the physician still holds in reserve."

"That might be the case with Dr. Svenson," Gina interjected, "but here at Children's Hospital we see numerous children who have terrible, incapacitating, even terminal illnesses. I am treating a fifteen-year-old boy who is a patient on the wards here. He has a progressive, painful, and incurable intestinal illness. I don't know what to do with him. All your life you treated patients other therapists had given up on, Dr. Bettelheim. What would you do in this case?"

"It is hard for me to be a mentor in such a case," Dr. B. said. "No matter what other therapists said, I always believed we might successfully treat any child we took into the Orthogenic School. For self-protective reasons, I always refused to work with patients I was convinced were incurable. I need to be hopeful myself to instill hope for themselves in my patients. While I admire people who can work with terminal cases, I just cannot convince myself that I would do well by them. So I choose not to work with them.

"Suppose I were treating your fifteen-year-old patient, and he asked me why he should want to live and what making 'progress' in psychotherapy would do for him? With his terrible illness, I would not know how to answer, unless he had something he wanted to do very badly and could do it before he became too debilitated. If all he wanted was to play games his body would not allow him to play, what could I say? Why should he struggle so hard to live? But I would not want him to give up, so I would be in a quandary, which would be of little help to this very ill boy."

"My response to him would be, 'If you don't struggle to live, you don't know what you'd be missing,'" Gina replied.

"That sounds upbeat and fortifying on the surface," I said. "And I would probably be tempted to say something similar. But I would be deceiving myself. Can you really say it with conviction? If the prognosis is accurate, what this boy will be missing is likely to be prolonged agony. You know it, I know it, and he probably suspects and fears it. Some clinicians find that helping people to 'die well' and not to be emotionally or spiritually alone is very meaningful work. They do an excellent job. But it's hard on you emotionally, so you have to feel good at that work, or you are not the right therapist for that individual."

No one in the seminar room liked hearing that, and the room was quiet for a time. Finally, Dr. B. spoke up. "As a therapist, you should treat only a person you feel you can give your best effort to. But this discussion reminds me of another context. What happens if a patient comes to you for treatment, and, for ethical reasons, you feel you cannot help with what this patient wishes to achieve? Such a situation arose in the Vienna Psychoanalytic Society during Naziism's early days. A member of the Vienna psychoanalytic group mentioned that an adherent of the Nazi party came to a gentile analyst, requesting the analyst's help in avoiding feeling guilt for beating up enemies of the Nazis, in particular Jews. He wanted to avoid these guilt feelings because he hoped to make a career in the party, and they stood in his way to political success.

"The society had a lively discussion in which quite a few members suggested that this analyst take the Nazi into therapy, because if the therapist succeeded, the patient would realize that he really did not want to be violently aggressive and might even comprehend the neurotic reasons that had led him to become a Nazi. Thus, he might become a solid citizen as a result of psychotherapy. Freud and some other senior members of the group objected to that approach. They felt that if one engaged in psychoanalysis with motives entirely opposite to the patient's unless the therapist declared this to the patient openly, the therapist would be starting the treatment with a lie, and no good would come of it. Of course, if the therapist explained what his different purposes were, as likely as not the patient would not enter treatment, or would start it feeling a great suspicion toward his therapist.

"Therefore, the only honest reply one can give such a patient is that since one is not in accord or sympathy with his reasons for entering psychotherapy, one chooses not to take him into therapy. That is the therapist's privilege, to decide whom one wants or does not want to treat. But the therapist has no right to accede silently to statements that are contrary to the therapist's convictions. The therapist has a right to choose how he spends his time and which kind of patient he wants to treat. If he accepts a patient for treatment, he should be in accord, if he can, with the reasons for which the patient seeks treatment. And if he cannot be, all the therapist can say is, 'I choose not to be involved.'"

The students looked at one another. Then Renee said. "But don't you have to take some stand as a therapist, have some belief about what is a right and a wrong way to live?"

"No," Dr. B. replied. "There we have the famous example of Socrates. He decided he had to live according to his daimon, the life he felt was the right one for him. And he was willing to die for it rather than to adapt himself for fitting in to Athenian society."

The group again was silent for a while. "Dr. Svenson's situation is very different from that of the unfortunate fifteen-year-old Gina described or from someone the therapist chooses not to treat," I said. "Dr. Svenson is in very good physical shape for an eighty year old, and Michael would like to help him, even though he is not a patient with fifty years ahead of him. With Dr. Svenson, the analogy to an internist's reassurance makes sense. The internist encourages his patient in order to give him confidence that the specific defect that needs to be remedied will be accessible to treatment. The same is true for the panic attacks Dr. Svenson suffers from. It's always good from time to time to counteract the patient's defeatism with reassurances regarding the positive aspects of his life."

"But should the reassurances come from the therapist?" Michael asked. "My trouble is that I can't decide whether I ought to reassure the patient."

"You have to listen to your mind and hear your heart to make that decision," I said. "Much of the impact reassurance makes will come from the way you do it. If you use your empathy to be sensitive to your patient's feelings and to the nuances of what reassurance might do for this individual, why he needs it and ought to have it at this moment in his treatment, you will be helpful and reassuring.

"But sometimes all of us are tempted to offer reassurance as a palliative. Then, what you hoped would reassure is very likely to have the opposite effect. Because, like the rest of us, when you are being evasive with a patient, you usually are not convincing. Perhaps you won't look the patient in the eyes, or you'll say things that sound insincere. The patient senses this and recognizes it for what it is. If the patient feels that your reassurance is a form of condescension, he will resent your low opinion or may feel you are avoiding telling him really grim news, for instance that he has what one patient called an 'emotional malignancy.' This will all frighten the patient more. But reassurance that really is consistent with how you view the patient and his or her situation will make an impression on your patient.

"The therapist also has to know himself well and why at this moment he wants to be reassuring. Is it really because it will help move therapy forward by bolstering a patient who needs it now? In a recent case, I realized that I was trying to reassure a patient at a particular moment because I wanted to reassure *myself* that the therapy was progressing adequately, even though, no, probably because, I had doubts about it. In that case, the reassurance really was aimed at making me, the therapist, feel better while disregarding the patient's needs.

"To be constructive to the patient, the therapist has to consider the patient's frame of mind, to assess how the patient will receive reassurances and react to them. Only then can we feel sure that our reassurances to the patient will serve positive purposes, and only then should we offer them."

Dr. B. picked up the thought. "In psychotherapy, the most persuasive reassurance comes from the positive experiences the patient has in treatment, with no need for you to underline them. For instance, if through his own efforts in psychotherapy, a man sees things he has done in a different light or understands things about himself that he previously had been unaware of, he is likely to feel encouraged about himself and enthusiastic about therapy. When a patient's understanding of himself grows, eventually he gains the courage to believe that he also can grow in other respects, such as in mastering reality in more positive ways.

"I cannot emphasize too much that the art of psychotherapy requires the ability to see and respect the patient's point of view. For example, to work in our field we see personal psychotherapy as indispensable and consider it the most constructive step a troubled person can take to overcome his problems. After all, every psychoanalytically oriented psychotherapist undergoes his own lengthy therapy or analysis. But if you listen to your patients or see them in your waiting room, you will see many who hide behind magazines or avert their gaze because they are ashamed to be there and do not want to be seen.

"Actually, many therapists also feel that way when they first enter their own treatment. With time, they discover how constructive psychotherapy is, and their attitudes change. But just because we feel that undergoing psychotherapy is a constructive step does not mean that the patient sees it that way right at the beginning. Also, therapists retain some other attitudes that reflect ambivalence about psychotherapy. While a dentist will maintain that his services are essential, psychotherapists often present their work as a luxury, a concept I do not agree with."

When everyone else remained silent, Michael said, "I don't want to leave the idea of reassurance so quickly. Wouldn't you consider the therapist who reassures a patient to be acting out?"

"Not if the reassurance is given correctly," Dr. B. replied. "Obviously the 'I'm okay, you're okay' is too facile, but mentioning some of your feelings to a patient, provided this helps therapy, may be very constructive. For example, it can be very useful to say to a patient at the end of a session—provided it is your honest impression—that he has worked very successfully at understanding his feelings about whatever was the issue of the hour and has made important steps forward in understanding himself around this issue. Such reassurance encourages the patient to think positively about himself, his intelligence and ability to understand himself, and his work in therapy in general.

"The difficulty Dr. Rosenfeld alluded to is that what reassures one patient, and makes him feel good about himself and optimistic about treatment, can make another patient distrustful because he experiences the words as empty talk. So even if he trusts the therapist fundamentally, he at least questions the therapist's good judgment. Another patient might take this encouragement as an effort to pressure him to do more than he feels capable of at the moment. In that case, the 'reassurance' would make the patient more dejected than he would have been had no reassurance been given. Furthermore, *any* patient may take a therapist's attempt at reassurance in any of these ways, depending on his mental state, the phase of treatment, and his relationship to his therapist. So you have to give careful thought to each case and situation."

"Should you talk about yourself and your feelings when you reassure?" Gina asked. "We hear so many different points of view on how open or mysterious you ought to be."

"Speaking about yourself as an individual, about aspects of your life, or the feelings that are evoked in you about what transpires in therapy is something you have to scrutinize carefully before doing. The reason the topic is so widely discussed is probably because it is so difficult to be sure that such comments are made solely for the patient's benefit, and not in part to meet your own needs. The patient has his hands more than full trying to meet his own needs, and, therefore, he should not be taken advantage of to satisfy *your* needs.

"But it's more than that. The patient needs to concentrate his entire attention on himself and what is going on in his mind. Any remark about your feelings will distract him from this task and direct him toward your person and *your* feelings, which he naturally is curious about to begin with. Hence, you inadvertently will seduce him into paying attention to you rather than to himself.

"Finally, as you know, the problem of transference plays an important role. The patient projects onto his therapist feelings that belong to other people or experiences in his past, such as feelings about his parents. His exploration of these feelings would become diluted, if not radically distorted, if at this point the therapist chose to interfere with remarks about his own feelings in the here and now. We need to be cognizant always that the feelings the patient projects onto us—such as his belief that we consider him worthless or beyond hope—can only be his projections, since he knows nothing about our real feelings. If we open up about our personal feelings, the patient will believe that he knows what we think and feel and will no longer recognize that his ideas about us are his projections. So I think that in most cases it is best that the patient know as little as possible about our own lives, or what goes on in us, unless our feelings have strictly to do with what transpires in therapy.

"Of course, psychoanalytic psychotherapy has no hard and fast rules besides the one that you must be honest with yourself and with your patients. So occasionally, it is quite all right to state your honest opinion if you are convinced that it will further treatment. Sometimes a statement about your own life, when appropriate, might be helpful. For example, if a patient asks you if you have children, it is not a bad idea, after you've asked why he wants to know, to give him a straight answer. There is always the chance that the patient might discover the answer and then resent you for holding a fact that otherwise would not interfere with treatment.

"I know that what I am saying differs from the idea that the analyst or therapist who bases treatment on psychoanalytic insight must be a blank screen in all situations. But I think that this rule of neutrality has its limitations. For example, a *New Yorker* article on psychoanalysis quoted an analyst who said that if his patient suddenly appeared for a session with a cast on her arm or leg, the correct attitude was for the analyst not to ask what happened until the patient told him. This does not seem correct to me or to many other analysts the author mentioned. A spontaneous reaction such as, 'My god! What happened to you?' is much more useful than a pretended indifference. Since we are all human beings, we all have human reactions, and the natural interest you have in your patient would induce you to ask such a question. Not to ask would signify casual indifference about what happened to your patient."

"Some analysts would say that with such a question, you are being seductive or intrusive," Jason said.

"I can't believe that a patient would consider the therapist's honest reaction as invading her privacy." I replied immediately. "You can't not act. Not doing something is as much an action as doing something. Therapist's often forget that. So if a patient coming in wearing a cast is a statement the patient makes, the therapist's reaction is the response. Some analysts feel that expressing sympathy will skew the patient's responses, so that the patient won't freely share *all* his feelings. To my way of thinking, neglecting to ask such a question when the patient obviously has suffered an injury is dishonest, and at least as deleterious as an intrusive question that does not stem from an obvious observation. When my response to your serious injury is silence, it can easily be perceived as indifference. And who here wants a therapist who is indifferent to your suffering?"

"I can agree with that," said Jason, "but wouldn't your sympathy stop her from exploring her motivation?"

"Not at all," I said. "Expressing your concern about this injury would not impede a psychoanalytic exploration of how it happened, because your concern includes wanting to hear every detail, conscious and unconscious. And that will help you find out the facts and move treatment forward."

"What if it turns out that this woman broke her arm because unconsciously she wanted your sympathy?" Bill said.

"When that became obvious," I said, "I would wonder along with her why she felt she had to go to such extreme lengths to get a warm or caring response from me."

"What if it turned out she did it because she needed to be punished for some success or pleasure?" Bill asked.

"Same difference. It all is grist for the mill," I said.

"Maybe an experience I had a long time ago with what gives reassurance and what does not will elucidate factors that may be involved," Dr. B. said. "I went into analysis a very long time ago, but after all these years I still recall what impressed me in my initial conversation with my analyst. The reason I contemplated entering psychoanalysis had to do with dissatisfactions concerning my private life and my vocation as a businessman, which I was at the time. Like many patients who are not in deep distress and who manage life reasonably well, I had doubts about whether I should enter psycho-analysis and whether it would benefit me. I spoke to the man who would become my analyst about my doubts and hesi-tations and asked him what he thought I should do. I asked him what psychoanalysis could do for me.

"To this, his reply (which, I'm sure, was based on his honest feelings) was: 'I do not know whether a man in your position needs analysis. I cannot promise what it will do for you, if for no other reason than because so much will depend on what you choose to do with what you may learn about your-self while undergoing analysis. But knowing a bit about you from what you have told me, and knowing also of your long-standing interest in psychoanalysis, I can promise that what you discover about yourself that you have not been aware of before will be very interesting to you.'

"He had spoken freely, and I felt truthfully, of his feelings about analysis. Both his refusal to decide whether I needed analysis and his promise that I would find it interesting con-vinced me to give it a try. Now in his heart, he might well have been convinced that analysis would do me a great deal of good. But I am quite sure that had he asserted that psy-choanalysis would do great things for me—things I badly needed—I would have felt such words to be empty reassur-ances about a matter on which I myself had serious doubts, and I would not have gone into analysis with him. I could not have put myself into the hands of a man I could not trust, and I would not have been able to trust a man when the outcome of things was plainly uncertain.

"So the combination of this therapist's refusal to reassure me about what analysis would do for me and his reassurance that I would find what I discovered about myself interesting made me trust him. What I am saying is that reassurance needs to be based not just on the analyst's conviction but also must be geared to the patient's needs at that moment in his life.

"To speak of my analysis for a moment longer," Dr. B. went on, "it is worth adding that during the analysis there were probably tremendous areas of mutual misunderstanding. But my analyst made an *effort* to understand, which was enough even if it may have misfired. We get an *E* for effort, not an *A* for achievement.

"In any analysis, my own included, increasing one's understanding, which is a goal of psychoanalysis, is only a means. The idea that it was an end is a mistaken notion that came from Freud's famous statement, 'Where there was id, there shall ego be,' which means that we should know what is going on in us. But even that is only a step. The ultimate goal of psychoanalysis is restructuring of the personality. For what purpose? So the person can live better with himself."

Everyone was silent for a time. Finally, I spoke. "I know we have digressed from discussing Dr. Svenson, but the point about reassurance seems so important that maybe we ought to go on with it a bit longer. Perhaps another example would help. Most therapists have seen children who tell them, 'I don't want to come here. I don't want to see you!' Reassuring such a boy, let's say, that therapy is for his own good and that he needs it is a true, accurate reflection of the therapist's conviction. But it would be counterproductive; it would set the therapist and child at cross-purposes. Most of all, it would be wrong because it disregards the child's fears, and it is those fears that make him refuse to enter treatment. Thus, such a comment fails to respect his feelings.

"But the therapist might, for example, tell the boy, 'It makes me very unhappy that you don't want to have anything to do with me; I will be very sad when you don't come back.' This response is somewhat theatric because it exaggerates the therapist's reactions if the child does not return, but young children like theatrics."

"Yes, they do," Dr. B. interjected. "After all, children are always on stage because they don't trust their own identity."

"They're constantly trying out new roles," I went on, "and this exaggerated response may be effective because, without giving what you normally would regard as reassurance, it addresses itself to the child's unhappy conviction that he is of no importance. This comment reassures the child that he is an important person who has the power to make people feel happy or unhappy. By indirectly referring to the child's power and influence, the therapist responds to the child's fear that in therapy he will be forced to do things against his desires and will be totally impotent. So in this case, words that by themselves contain no reassurance at all can be the most reassuring thing a therapist can say.

"But Michael's problem is how to help an old man return to the world of the living. If Dr. Svenson does this, much of his disappointment and rage, with which he now attacks himself and which results in his panicking, will mitigate. This easing up may come perhaps through his offering to others —in effect, surrogates for his son—some teaching about orthopedic surgery, to which he has devoted his life and thereby found pleasure. That also might allow him to reestablish his relationship to his wife on a positive basis, which means they both will have more pleasure in their remaining years."

"Do we have time for a question?" Gina asked.

Both Dr. B. and I nodded.

"Your remark brought to mind a difficult problem of psychoanalytic theory that I've been struggling with," Gina said. "I've been reading a lot about Freud's theory of Eros and Thanatos," she said. "Do you think the death instinct plays a role in Dr. Svenson's symptoms?"

"That is an erroneous interpretation of the *death instinct*, or the death *drive* to use a better term," Dr. B. answered. "Nobody really wants to die; that is our destiny. It's the burden of individuality we want to lay down.

"You know, when Winston Churchill was a very old man, he was once told that his zipper was open. And he said, 'Never mind. The dead bird doesn't leave the nest.' I don't want you to think we old men are entirely dead or don't regret it if our sex life is. So even though this doctor is a bit old for the example I'll give, let me use it anyway.

"The death drive plays an essential role in sexual excitement and its peak. The experience of orgasm momentarily removes our ego boundaries; in it we temporarily lose our individuality and merge with the other. And after coitus, as the Romans said, there is sadness and exhaustion. So in orgasm, for a moment we are free from ego boundaries, which in a way is the death of the individual."

"But that loss of individuality is intensely pleasurable," Michael said.

"That's right," Dr. B. said. "There is a tremendous relief in not having to do the hard work we constantly perform to maintain our ego's boundaries."

"I also think that some people have to make a great effort just to maintain a brittle and rigid personality," I said. "Therefore, they cannot allow themselves to be sexually excited because that threatens to disintegrate their personality."

"But I am thinking that so many people seek sexual arousal compulsively," Dr. B. went on. "Keeping our personality intact takes great effort, and when we are temporarily relieved of this necessity, it can be intensely pleasurable. However, as you say, a person who fears he won't be able to reestablish his ego boundaries after they have momentarily dissolved may need to retain rigid control and is unable to merge himself into the other.

"When people say they wish to go back to nature, mother earth, or whatever poetic image they use, they imply that they wish the burden of their individuality to be at least temporarily relieved. When it is, they merge their individuality into something bigger. Insofar as in this experience a person's individuality disappears, we may speculate that the death drive has a role in it. And of course, it also comes in when we consider man's destructive tendencies."

Gina spoke up. "When you talk that way, you sound so pessimistic, like these drives are railroad tracks that people are put on, and their lives will follow that course no matter what."

"You are asking about a large issue we can only touch on," Dr. B. replied. "You are really asking what Freud thought the therapy he invented could achieve. And there's some truth in your disappointment. Although Freud believed that some of man's aspects could be changed somewhat, he saw others as intractable, problems that arose out of man's very nature. So in contrast to many who promise Utopia, Freud had a far less optimistic view."

Renee jumped in. "Given the choice, I personally would choose to be optimistic, wouldn't you?"

"Certainly," Dr. B. said. "Provided your optimism is reasoned and well founded. The contrast between Freud and those who promise nirvana is not between pessimism and optimism, but between what is possible, given man's limitations, and what really is a utopian, unachievable vision.

"But I disagree with your calling Freud 'pessimistic.' He had an optimistic view, albeit a guarded one, of what psychoanalysis can do for individuals. He was convinced that the psychoanalysis he had invented would be a great step forward in understanding ourselves and also, when correctly applied, others. He even thought that his psychoanalysis could free man of some of his most crippling inhibitions, such as those we have about sex.

"Freud's influence in this area has been so pervasive that we can easily overlook how indebted we are to him for his optimism about what could be achieved in respect to a more open, honest, truly intimate sexual attitude, and all that is connected to it. He was optimistic about the benefits for mankind if instead of repressing sexuality, people accepted it as natural. You almost could say he created the possibility for freer sexual relations between men and women and an atmosphere in which previously tabooed topics, such as homosexuality and abortion, could be discussed.

"Freud maintained a limited optimism about what psychoanalysis could achieve for individuals. He said that it could, and ought to, free patients from self-created pain and hardships, but he felt that ultimately the suffering and pain originating in our very nature as humans could not be avoided. Therefore, success in psychoanalysis was limited to a patient's learning to distinguish which sufferings were self-inflicted, and thus could be avoided, and which were not; then the individual could develop the ability to bear the latter with fortitude.

"Freud was much less optimistic—if not outright pessimistic—about the potential for changing man's aggressive tendencies. In his correspondence with Einstein, he countered Einstein's hopes about war and peace with a reasoned pessimism. However, when the Nazis burned his books, Freud retained a shred of optimism and remarked that, in times past, he himself would have been burned.

"Freud did not live long enough to realize that even this very mild and limited optimism about man's aggressive tendencies turned out to be in error. A few years after he died, the Nazis did burn people by the hundreds of thousands, including Freud's own sister. And, of course, today the hydrogen bomb threatens to be much more devastatingly destructive to mankind. Overall, then, we must say that psychoanalytic optimism is optimism within narrowly drawn limits.

"Thus one might say that Freud's goal was a limited, well-tempered optimism, and a skepticism kept within well-controlled bounds that would not interfere with one's ability 'to love well and to work well.' Freud regarded these abilities not only as the desirable outcome of psychoanalysis but as characteristic of the well-integrated person."

With this, we ended the session. We had covered so many topics, yet so much remained unsaid. But we ended with the hope that through Michael Simpson's sincere efforts, one old man would rediscover his value, restore himself to emotional health, and find pleasure in the time left to him. Michael would gain too. For he would learn from Dr. Svenson, would be allowed to share in an old man's experience of and struggle with old age. The experience would be likely to enrich both of them.

EPILOGUE

AT THE TIME Bruno Bettelheim and I were engaged in editing the transcripts that eventually became this book, we gave it the working title "In the Shoes of a Stranger." The title reflected the central message we wished to convey: that for a therapist, empathy is the most crucial working tool. In the course of editing the book after Dr. B.'s death, however, I came to perceive a more general, and perhaps even more valuable, sort of understanding that this extraordinary teacher sought to pass on to a new generation—what he called, with a kind of sly understatement, "the art of the obvious." By this he meant the art of seeing clearly what is there to be seen, rather than imposing on it one's own presuppositions and prejudices.

Although we spent most of our time in the seminars speaking about child psychotherapy, the attitudes, techniques, and approaches that we discussed have considerable applicability in the treatment of adults as well. To some degree, the ideas and dilemmas that we grappled with in these seminars also have application to the art of our everyday human relationships.

In an age when calibration and direct measurement are increasingly considered the only true pathways to knowledge, calling psychoanalytically oriented psychotherapy "an art" is fraught with risk; to many, it may imply that clinical practice is haphazard, unscholarly, imprecise, and hopelessly subjective. In actuality, "the art of the obvious" implies that for the psychotherapist to see what is there in front of him requires more than empathy and emotional receptivity; it calls for humility, patience, a reflective attitude, and long study to master both theory and technique.

Some years ago, I saw a remarkable television interview that Dick Cavett conducted with Isaac Stern. During their conversation, Stern, at Cavett's request, picked up a violin and played an arpeggio. It was so full of feeling, so smooth and perfect, that Cavett and his audience were stunned. Stern then played the arpeggio again, with the notes separated by perhaps a quarter of a second. He played it a dozen more times; each time the notes were fractionally closer, until they once again became a seamless whole again. "How did you do that?" demanded Cavett, astonished. Stern began to talk about how he had practiced six hours a day for twenty-five years, until the muscles in his hands were extremely strong and completely under his command. He grew reflective for a moment, and then said that because he had achieved absolute control of his instrument, he felt comfortable being completely spontaneous. "When I perform," Stern said, "all I pay attention to is my feelings."

Of course, if Stern had not achieved such superb mastery of his instrument, of his craft, and of himself as an artist, his "spontaneous" performance, however full of feeling, might have sounded dreadful. In much the same way, every psychotherapist must spend years getting the technical training that forms the foundation of his craft, in order to be able to pay proper attention to his feelings, observations, and intuitions about patients. Seasoned practitioners take great pleasure in practicing psychotherapy and psychoanalysis, because the learning never stops. Each new patient helps the experienced clinician see new, unique aspects of human experience and the human condition.

I believe that a psychodynamic psychotherapist's training ought to be broad and eclectic. Students must know about the stages of normal human development and about psychopathology. They need considerable life experience, and preferably first-hand knowledge about the suffering, traumas, and losses that people endure and by which they are shaped, and which will color forever after the way they see the world and life's meaning. In this process, the therapist's experiences and humble understanding that "There, but for the grace of God, go I" is the basis for genuine empathy with patients.

Any psychotherapist needs to be flexible in his approach to patients, to respect the different approaches, not all of them necessarily psychodynamic, that can be useful in different circumstances. Furthermore, therapists must become skilled in recognizing true organic and neurological damage, and appreciating which patients may not be treatable with psychoanalytic techniques. Even in these cases, however, a psychoanalytic perspective may help the therapist design a sensitive approach to the patient.

Psychotherapy students need to know when psychotropic medications are appropriate and useful and when they are not. They need to appreciate the importance of life events and the power that nourishing human relationships can have to heal psychological wounds. Too often, drugs are prescribed to reduce the therapist's own anxiety with a patient rather than to serve a patient's needs.

Psychotherapy does not have the elegant precision of Newtonian physics. Students who want to take a psychodynamic approach must tolerate ambiguity and uncertainty. They must be willing to encounter and even encourage intense emotions, pain, passions, and rage, and must wrestle with the anxiety and distortion these feelings introduce into the therapeutic relationship. Finally, they must understand that change in psychotherapy can be haltingly slow, and not allow a seeming lack of progress to discourage them.

Perhaps most important, therapists must develop their own personality and feelings into therapeutic instruments. To do this they must become intimate with themselves, to explore their own drives, passions, sentiments, fears, hopes, and wishes. They need to come to terms not just with their wish to help, but with their less benevolent desires, such as the impulse to influence or dominate another.

Psychotherapy is always an interaction. The therapist, no matter how skilled, cannot succeed alone. Good ideas and a clear perspective on a patient's problems are essential, but they alone cannot make a patient better. For that, the patient's deep desire to get well is a crucial factor.

Behavior is purposeful. The therapist's first task is to decode the messages implicit in behavior by listening carefully to what the patient says and by watching what he does. If a patient is aggressive, what might be his intent and against whom or what might he be reacting? The therapist ought to ask, "What would I be trying to achieve if I behaved that way? How would I *hope* the people around me, my therapist included, would react?" The patient needs to see that his therapist believes he has good reasons for his behavior; that often will help make the patient more interested in reflecting on his motivation and goals.

Since behavior is a communication, the therapist's own behavior is a crucial factor in what happens during treatment. The patient, even a very damaged individual like Luke in Dan Berenson's research project, responds to the therapist's actions, not just to inner pressures. It would be hard to emphasize too strongly how sensitive both a diagnostician and/ or a therapist should be to the messages he is giving, in both words and actions.

It is worth pointing out that the parents of an emotionally or psychologically troubled child need empathy too. I think that Dr. B., despite his brilliance, was so committed to children that he sometimes did not appreciate sufficiently a parent's pain. Today's psychotherapists need to comprehend how hard it is to be a parent and how deeply parents' hearts can break, how frightened, disappointed, and angry they can get when they find that their child is ill, whether physically or emotionally.

Bruno Bettelheim experienced in his own person the degradation and disintegration that the concentration camp experience elicited. That experience gave him firsthand knowledge of the way trauma impacts on the human psyche. He saw what each of us can become, how we can be deformed by exposure to extreme conditions. His experience in the camps had, he said, a strong role in committing him to the "rescue" of severely disturbed children. He devoted the last fifty years of his life to that end.

Bettelheim believed, as I do, that we are all alike in one most fundamental way, in our need to be loved and cared for, and that each of us is worthy of respect. We both believe that children need to be indulged and nurtured; his principle of treating a patient as you would an honored guest in your home seems particularly valid in an age when psychiatric patients are so often treated as diagnostic specimens to be correctly classified in some sort of Linnaean system. Clinicians with this approach often do not see that their distant, detached stance can cause pain and influence the behavior they think they are neutrally observing.

Respecting the individual and paying careful attention to the patient's thoughts, feelings, and actions form the backbone of the psychodynamic therapeutic process. The patient has to come to the conclusion—one that he arrives at independently by watching what his therapist does and listening to what he says—that his therapist is an ally who is trying to help him get what he wants from life. As the patient repeatedly has the experience that the therapist is on his side, he will begin to pay more attention to and take seriously the therapist's comments, suggestions, and interventions.

Psychotherapy is hard enough even under the best of circumstances, filled with difficult, painful insights into oneself.

The patient needs to feel that he is gaining these new insights in a supportive, respectful atmosphere, with someone who wants to help him find the courage to make major changes in his view of the world, changes that the patient himself decides are in his best interest, and that will enable him to live more comfortably with himself. Only with such support and understanding can the patient muster that courage.

As we worked on this book, Bruno Bettelheim and I were often aware of the poignant similarities between him and Dr. Svenson. Both men had distinguished careers, but had ceased to be actively involved in their life's work; both were suffering the emotional consequences. When Dr. B. advised Michael Simpson to draw Dr. Svenson back into some meaningful relationship to the world, he clearly also had himself in mind.

It was in this spirit that the present work was created. It is intended as a living testament to my friendship with Bruno Bettelheim, and to the way one old man added meaning to his later years by sharing what he knew with younger psychotherapists. The process of knowing and working intimately with Bettelheim has enriched my life immeasurably. I hope that with this volume I will in some measure pass on the creative legacy of an extraordinary human being and the wisdom he entrusted to me in his final years.

INDEX

abuse, sexual, 5
see also children, abused; incest;
    sexual abuse
abused children, see children,
    abused
adults, treatment of, 231
aggressiveness, 84–6
    in case of abused child (Bobby),
        97–8
    in case of autistic child (Luke),
        105–11
    in case of child with learning
        disability (Eduardo), 146–
        65
    Freud's views on, 229
aging, problems of, 211–12
    psychotherapy for, 202–3
    see also elderly patient case
agoraphobia, 192–4, 195,
    198
American Psychiatric Association,
    see DSM III
anal concerns, 178–81
analysis, see psychoanalysis; psy-
    chotherapy, psychoanalyti-
    cally oriented
anorexia nervosa
    case study (Margot), 41–64
    case treated at Orthogenic
        School, 56–8
anxieties
    of patient, 29, 35, 48–9, 61,
        204–5
    of therapist, 29, 35, 48–9, 61,
        98–9, 102, 129, 135, 143

Archives of General Psychiatry,
    116
"art of the obvious," 11, 81,
    231–2
autism, see children, autistic

babyhood, Dr. B.'s view of, 7
behavior
    as communication, 234
    context/meaning in, 66–7, 68,
        97, 107–8, 131–2, 138,
        158, 163–4, 234
    normal, 35
    observing, 27–8, 32–4
behaviorism, 15–16, 80, 199, 204
behavior therapy
    vs. insight-oriented work,
        15–16, 204
    limitations of, 74
    as treatment model, 73–4
Bettelheim, Dr. Bruno
    approach to teaching, 6–12
    concentration camp experience
        of, 16, 80–1, 89, 235
    controversies about, 4, 18, 22
    death of, 20–2
    description of, 4, 7–8, 188
    and incurable cases, 215–17
    and milieu therapy, 17
    at Orthogenic School, 17–18,
        22
    personal analysis of, 223–5

A NOTE
ABOUT THE
AUTHORS

BRUNO BETTELHEIM was born in Vienna in 1903. He received his doctorate at the University of Vienna, and came to America in 1939, after a year in the concentration camps of Dachau and Buchenwald. He was Distinguished Professor of Education Emeritus and Professor Emeritus of both psychology and psychiatry at the University of Chicago. His previous books include *Children of the Dream, The Informed Heart, Love Is Not Enough, A Home for the Heart, Surviving and Other Essays, Freud and Man's Soul,* and *A Good Enough Parent.* In 1977, he won both the National Book Award and the National Book Critics Circle Award for *The Uses of Enchantment.* Dr. Bettelheim died in 1990.

DR. ALVIN A ROSENFELD practices adult, adolescent, and child psychiatry in New York City, and directs Psychiatric Services at the Jewish Child Care Association. Educated and trained at Harvard Medical School, he was on the faculty there and was later director of child psychiatry training at Stanford University Medical School. He is the author of over sixty professional publications and three books: *The Somatizing Child* (with Dr. Elsa Shapiro), *Healing the Heart* (with Dr. Saul Wasserman), and a novel, *A Dissenter in the House of God.*

A Note on the Type

The text of this book was set in Sabon, a
typeface designed by Jan Tschichold (1902–1974),
the well-known German typographer. Based loosely
on the original designs of Claude Garamond
(c. 1480–1561), Sabon is unique in that it was
explicitly designed for hot-metal composition on
both the Monotype and Linotype machines as well
as for film setting. Designed in Frankfurt,
Sabon was named for the famous Lyon punchcutter
Jacques Sabon, who is thought to have brought some
of Garamond's matrices to Frankfurt.

Composed by PennSet, Inc., Bloomsburg, Pennsylvania
Printed and bound by Haddon Craftsmen,
Scranton, Pennsylvania
Designed by Anthea Lingeman